11+ English

Multiple-choice Test Papers
Pack 1
The secrets of 11+ success

OXFORD
UNIVERSITY PRESS

Great Clarendon Street, Oxford, OX2 6DP, United Kingdom

Oxford University Press is a department of the University of Oxford. It furthers the University's objective of excellence in research, scholarship, and education by publishing worldwide. Oxford is a registered trade mark of Oxford University Press in the UK and in certain other countries

Text © Sarah Lindsay 2015
Illustrations © Oxford University Press 2015

The moral rights of the authors have been asserted

First published in 2015

All rights reserved. No part of this publication may be reproduced, stored in a retrieval system, or transmitted, in any form or by any means, without the prior permission in writing of Oxford University Press, or as expressly permitted by law, by licence or under terms agreed with the appropriate reprographics rights organization. Enquiries concerning reproduction outside the scope of the above should be sent to the Rights Department, Oxford University Press, at the address above.

You must not circulate this work in any other form and you must impose this same condition on any acquirer

British Library Cataloguing in Publication Data
Data available

978-0-19-274083-0

Paper used in the production of this book is a natural, recyclable product made from wood grown in sustainable forests. The manufacturing process conforms to the environmental regulations of the country of origin.

Printed in China

Acknowledgements

The publishers would like to thank the following for permissions to use copyright material:

Cover illustrations: Lo Cole

Although we have made every effort to trace and contact all copyright holders before publication this has not been possible in all cases. If notified, the publisher will rectify any errors or omissions at the earliest opportunity.

Links to third party websites are provided by Oxford in good faith and for information only. Oxford disclaims any responsibility for the materials contained in any third party website referenced in this work.

The secrets of 11+ success in English

How 11+ exams work

Approaching 11+ exams for the first time can be a daunting experience. They are unlike any other school exam your child will take for several reasons:

- *There's no pass mark.* Success or failure depends on your child's performance relative to the performance of other children sitting the test. The pass mark can vary from year to year and from school to school.

- *They can't be retaken.* There is no second chance with the 11+ so it all rests on your child's performance on the day.

- *There's no national syllabus.* 11+ exams vary from area to area, and often from town to town. Often schools are extremely unwilling to give out any information about the content of the exams.

- *It's often impossible to see past papers.* This varies from area to area but the actual papers usually remain a closely guarded secret. However, schools will often make a sample English paper available to parents.

- *Selective schools give out very little advice.* It is common for selective schools to give out only the vaguest advice to parents when approaching the exam and to discourage very much practice.

All these factors make preparing a child for the 11+ a mysterious and often stressful process for parent and child alike. The most common question parents ask about using practice tests is 'What percentage does my child need to get to pass?' Unfortunately there's no easy answer to this but we can give guidance (see 'What a score means and how to boost it' on page 3). The second most common question is 'How can I help them improve?' The following sections give our tutors' top tips to help your child through the 11+ process and boost their scores. We strongly recommend that you think about purchasing some other essential Bond resources.

- *The Parents' Guide to the 11+*. The essential manual that provides a simple and practical 4-step system for making the most of 11+ preparation.

- *How To Do 11+ English.* All the English skills tested in these papers are explored in more detail in this guide to 11+ English.

- *Focus on Comprehension* and *Focus on Writing*. Most 11+ English exams involve a comprehension exercise and many also include at least one writing task. These books provide vital support for these key aspects of 11+ English preparation.

Tutors' top tips for 11+ success

- *Find out what exams your child will sit but don't agonise over 'school-gate gossip'.* Find out what the exams are and get the advice that the secondary schools give out, but don't waste your energy following rumours about what the pass mark is. It's better to spend your time helping your child.

- *It's always worth practising.* Whatever secondary schools say, it's worth it. Children can improve their performance by 10–15% by careful practice.

- *Start early if you can, but don't worry if you haven't.* Ideally it is best to start preparation for the 11+ exam at least one year ahead. However, don't panic if you don't have that much time; even a few weeks can make a difference.

- *Make a simple action plan.* However long you've got, have a clear, simple strategy. There are two key principles:
  - start from your child's present level of knowledge
  - help your child to learn from their mistakes.

  The Parents' Guide to the 11+ provides a set of ready-made action plans you can use, whether you have two years or just a few weeks to go.

- *Motivation, motivation, motivation!* You have to take your child with you on this journey. A simple rewards system can be highly effective. *The Parents' Guide to the 11+* can provide a tried and tested motivational system if you want one.

- *Don't just practise.* There's a tendency to think that just practising one paper after another will do the trick. It's far more important to learn from mistakes. Going through the paper afterwards with your child and filling in the gaps in learning is crucial.

- *Stay calm, manage stress, build confidence.* Don't talk about the 11+ all the time. Use breaks, treats and bite-sized learning sessions to keep things fresh. Be realistic about your child's potential. Pass or fail, it's important to try to make this process a positive one.

- *Manage the exam day.* Make sure that you have everything ready for the day, that your child tries to get a good night's sleep, eats breakfast and gets there in good time.

How and when to use these tests

- *It's best to use them as real exam practice.* These tests are mock exams. They are set out in a style as close as possible to the real thing – though the format will vary from area to area. It is best to use them as authentic exam experience rather than for general practice, and to use them quite close to the exam. Follow the instructions in the answers booklet on timings and administering the test papers and writing tasks.

What's in an 11+ English exam?

Most of the English skills your child will need to draw on for an 11+ exam will be a continuation of those being developed in literacy at school. Some of the questions on the 11+ papers may be set at a higher level than your child has come across before, but they will be testing the same range of knowledge and skills. The content and structure of 11+ English papers can differ greatly from one school to the next, but a paper will generally test your child's knowledge of, and skills in:

- comprehension
- grammar
- punctuation
- spelling
- extended writing.

Comprehension

Strong comprehension skills are crucial for success in 11+ English exams, as most test papers include at least one comprehension task. Some papers can be based completely around a comprehension text; subsequently, the comprehension exercise could carry up to 100% of the total available marks.

On average, a child will have about 50 minutes to complete an English paper and may be asked to answer questions that require them to find, select or reorganise information in the text as well as provide answers based on personal knowledge, interpretation or opinion. Responses may need to be presented in a range of formats, e.g. selection of the correct multiple-choice option, one word or a short phrase, a few lines or a more lengthy explanation written in several paragraphs (for more details about 11+ comprehension tasks and the skills and strategies involved, see 'The English your child needs for the 11+ exam' on page 4, *Focus on Comprehension* and *How To Do 11+ English*).

Grammar, punctuation and spelling

Sound English skills are underpinned by knowledge of the rules relating to grammar, punctuation and spelling. As a result, an 11+ English exam will test a child's understanding in these fundamental areas. Questions based on these core elements of language may be included within the main comprehension exercise, or they may form a separate section that is unrelated to the comprehension text (for more details about these key aspects of English, as well as strategies for tackling them, see 'The English your child needs for the 11+ exam' on page 4 and *How To Do 11+ English*).

Extended writing

Most 11+ English exams include at least one writing task. This may form a section within a combined paper that also tests the other skills areas listed above, or it may be set as a separate writing paper.

Some schools will set a writing task but it may not be marked unless a child's total is borderline with the qualifying score. Where a writing task is taken into account for the overall score, it can carry up to 50% of the total 11+ English marks. The time frame for a writing task can differ depending on the individual school and style of paper, but usually a minimum of 30 minutes is given.

Typically, a child will have to choose one or two questions to answer from a selection of options. Questions can be based on a wide range of themes or writing styles, for example:

- a factual essay or description
- a piece of fictional narrative or descriptive writing
- a formal/informal letter or diary entry
- a debate
- a continuation of a piece of given text
- a composition based on a visual stimulus such as a photograph.

(For more details about 11+ writing tasks and the skills and strategies involved, see 'The English your child needs for the 11+ exam' on page 4, *Focus on Writing*, *How To Do 11+ English* and *Focus on Comprehension*).

What a score means and how to boost it

It is unfortunately impossible to say that a certain score can guarantee a pass in the actual exams. However, we suggest that a score of 85% (42/50 for each test paper and 17/20 for each writing task enclosed) would be a standard to aim at. It is important not to present this to your child as a concrete benchmark though, as the best motivator for them is to see the scores going up. Here are some tried and tested tips for improvement:

- *Go over any incorrect answers.* Always go over incorrect answers so that your child can see what went wrong. To help with this process, the answers in these test papers are explained and also have individual tutorial reference icons: B1 . This icon links to the relevant section in *How To Do 11+ English* so your child can read more about the related topic and complete additional practice activities if needed.

- *Use the Next Steps Planner inside the back cover.* This will provide a plan for what to do next when a test has been marked.

- *Improve basic exam technique.* Work on improving speed, working efficiently – coming back to trickier questions later – and pacing within the time limit.

- *Improve general English skills.* Ensure the foundations are strong enough. Use the range of checklists below to help reinforce your child's English skills.

- *Target what is not fully understood.* The secret is not to keep blindly practising but to target the areas of English that your child is weakest in. This is where crucial marks can be picked up.

The English your child needs for 11⁺ exams

Below is a set of brief checklists that highlight the key knowledge and essential skills your child will need for the five main aspects of English (for more details on these five areas, the skills required and for further practice activities, see *How To Do 11⁺ English*, *Focus on Comprehension* and *Focus on Writing*). To further underpin each of these key areas, encourage your child to read as widely as possible. Extensive reading is one of the best ways of improving word, grammar and spelling knowledge, as well as supporting comprehension and writing skills.

Comprehension

Comprehension exercises can involve a wide range of skills. Talk about comprehension tasks with your child and check that they can:

- understand and retrieve information
- summarise part of a text
- infer, interpret and predict a plot line
- place a text in context (e.g. historical, cultural or social)
- comment on a writer's aim and/or viewpoint
- comment on the organisation and structure used
- explain a writer's use of language
- support answers by quoting from the text
- demonstrate knowledge of vocabulary, spelling and syntax.

Support your child's comprehension skills by making sure they know how to:

- find vital clues in a text
- recognise different text types
- identify different question types
- check their answers.

Grammar and punctuation

For 11⁺ English, your child needs to have sound foundations in the core aspects of grammar and punctuation. In particular, it will be valuable to check that they understand how to:

- recognise and use parts of speech (e.g. nouns, pronouns, verbs, adjectives, adverbs, prepositions, subjects and objects)
- structure phrases, clauses, sentences and paragraphs
- use common punctuation marks (e.g. apostrophes, commas, full stops, question marks, exclamation marks, colons and semi-colons)
- write dialogue (both in the form of direct and reported speech)
- identify and form compound words, synonyms, antonyms, similes, metaphors, abbreviations, acronyms, gender forms and diminutives.

Spelling

As your child's spelling skills will also be assessed in an 11⁺ English exam, it will be valuable to check that they are able to:

- recognise and spell common letter strings
- form singulars and plurals
- attach prefixes and suffixes
- identify and spell homophones and homonyms
- spot silent letters and unstressed vowels.

Spellings should be practised regularly in order to build confidence. Therefore, try to ensure that your child:

- learns their weekly spelling list from school
- knows the key spelling rules (e.g. 'i' before 'e' except after c)
- is aware of their most common spelling errors
- can use a dictionary and thesaurus and refers to both regularly
- uses a range of techniques to practise (e.g. 'Look, Say, Cover, Write, Check'; creating mnemonics for difficult spellings; playing word games such as Scrabble® or completing daily spelling challenges using a spelling list.

Writing

Strong writing skills form the basis for so many exams and particularly for tests which involve specific writing tasks. The focus of these tasks could be pretty much anything, so your child will have to draw on a wide range of knowledge and skills. Try to give constructive feedback on your child's writing and check that they can:

- write legibly and fluently
- write imaginatively in a range of forms (e.g. narrative, playscript, report, letter)
- adapt their writing style to suit the task (e.g. writing to inform, persuade, argue etc.)
- engage and entertain a reader
- plan, organise and develop ideas effectively
- understand the differences between standard and non standard English
- construct simple/complex sentences to create reading effects
- draw on an extended vocabulary and use accurate spelling
- use all parts of speech and punctuation marks correctly (see above).

11+ English

Multiple-choice Test Papers
Pack 1
Notes and Answers

This booklet contains:

- advice on how to administer the tests
- answers
- tutors' explanations for every answer
- links to **How To Do English**

OXFORD
UNIVERSITY PRESS

Great Clarendon Street, Oxford, OX2 6DP, United Kingdom

Oxford University Press is a department of the University of Oxford. It furthers the University's objective of excellence in research, scholarship, and education by publishing worldwide. Oxford is a registered trade mark of Oxford University Press in the UK and in certain other countries

Text © Sarah Lindsay 2015
Illustrations © Oxford University Press 2015

The moral rights of the authors have been asserted

First published in 2015

All rights reserved. No part of this publication may be reproduced, stored in a retrieval system, or transmitted, in any form or by any means, without the prior permission in writing of Oxford University Press, or as expressly permitted by law, by licence or under terms agreed with the appropriate reprographics rights organization. Enquiries concerning reproduction outside the scope of the above should be sent to the Rights Department, Oxford University Press, at the address above.

You must not circulate this work in any other form and you must impose this same condition on any acquirer

British Library Cataloguing in Publication Data
Data available

978-0-19-274083-0

Paper used in the production of this book is a natural, recyclable product made from wood grown in sustainable forests. The manufacturing process conforms to the environmental regulations of the country of origin.

Printed in China

Acknowledgements

The publishers would like to thank the following for permissions to use copyright material:

Cover illustrations: Lo Cole

Although we have made every effort to trace and contact all copyright holders before publication this has not been possible in all cases. If notified, the publisher will rectify any errors or omissions at the earliest opportunity.

Links to third party websites are provided by Oxford in good faith and for information only. Oxford disclaims any responsibility for the materials contained in any third party website referenced in this work.

How to administer the tests

What's in the pack?

This pack contains four mock test papers that will help you to assess comprehension skills alongside elements of grammar, punctuation and spelling knowledge. A separate sheet of four writing tasks, which provides key practice of writing skills, is also included.

What do you need?

- A quiet, well-lit place to sit each test.
- A stock of pencils. HB pencils are best for multiple-choice papers.
- A pencil sharpener and an eraser.
- Blank paper for rough working.
- A clock or timer.

Setting the test papers

1. Before you start

Try to provide a calm yet formal atmosphere in which your child can take the test. It is important that you recreate the real test as closely as possible, so try to ensure your child has an appropriate work space and no distractions. Choose a time to do a test when your child is rested and relaxed.

Multiple-choice tests ask children to mark their answers in a separate answer booklet. Therefore, when reading the front page of the test paper with your child, point out the importance of answering carefully and rubbing out any altered answers clearly (read the section below for details of common pitfalls that can occur when using multiple-choice answer booklets). Ensure that enough rough paper is available for working out answers; they should not use the empty space on the paper for workings.

Allow 50 minutes per test. On average, they will have one minute to answer each question, so encourage them to move on from questions they are stuck on before too much time is wasted. Your child may find it helpful to put a cross in pencil by questions that have been missed out so that they can be quickly spotted later on. Remind them that they can always go back at the end if they have time left. Finish reading the instructions together, and then allow them five minutes to read the comprehension text before you 'start the clock'.

When the time is up they should stop writing. If they have not finished, draw a line at the point they have reached. You can always allow them to continue after the time to get more practice, or else leave the other questions blank for another day. Encourage them to think about whether they should try to speed up, or to work more carefully, depending on how they finish the paper.

2. Using the multiple-choice answer booklet

If your child is sitting a multiple-choice exam it is crucial that they understand how to use the answer booklet properly. Spend time examining the booklet together. As you look through it explain that multiple-choice answer sheets are usually scored by computer rather than by hand, (an optical reader scans the marks on each page). As a result, an answer will be classed as wrong if it is not clearly and accurately marked.

There are some common mistakes that are easy to make when using a multiple-choice answer booklet. Talk through the following points carefully with your child, without panicking them, but so that they understand exactly what they should / should not do:

- *Marking outside the box.* To record an answer, a clear line should be made through the centre of the relevant answer box. The line should stay within the border of the box so that it can be read accurately by the computer.

- *Crossing out an answer.* If your child wants to change their mind they must never cross out an answer in a multiple-choice booklet. It must be fully rubbed out and then the new answer should be clearly marked in the appropriate box. If any mark is left in the first box, the computer could read two answers for that question and mark their response as incorrect.

- *Marking an answer in the wrong grid.* Answer grids often look the same on multiple-choice answer sheets so it is easy to mark an answer in the wrong grid, which can have a knock-on effect for all successive answers. Encourage your child to check that the question number of the grid matches the question they are answering before they make each mark. They should also take extra care if they decide to miss out a question to return to later.

- *Not pressing hard enough.* If a mark is too light, it may not be recognised by the computer and the question could be marked wrong. Remind your child that each answer needs to be marked clearly. We would suggest practising with soft HB pencils as they tend to make the clearest marks. If your child has to provide their own pencils for the actual test, make sure they take one or two HB pencils with them.

3. Marking and feedback

The answers that follow should be given one mark unless otherwise indicated. Do not take marks away for wrong answers, but do not award half marks. You will end up with a score out of 50. Double the score to get a percentage. 42/50 equals the target score of 85% (see 'The secrets of 11⁺ success in English' booklet).

After marking, follow these steps:

- *Go over any incorrect answers.* Always go over incorrect answers so that your child can see what went wrong. To help with this process, the answers in these test papers are explained and also have individual tutorial reference icons: [B1]. This icon links to the relevant section in *How To Do 11⁺ English* so your child can read more about the related topic and try some more practice activities if needed.

- *Use the Next Steps Planner inside the back cover.* This will provide a plan for what to do next when a test has been marked.

Setting the writing tasks

It is also important to recreate the exam experience when setting a writing task, so try to ensure your child has a quiet place to complete each exercise. Only one task should be completed at a time and they can be written in pencil or pen, whichever your child feels most comfortable with. As the writing tasks are based on the four comprehension texts (one in each test paper), the relevant extract should be read before each task is attempted. Allow up to ten minutes for this.

A word limit has been set for each task to enable children to practise writing concisely and a suggested time frame of 30 minutes has also been given. If you want your child to practise writing at speed, try reducing the time limit by five minutes but still allow up to ten minutes' additional reading time. Your child may find it helpful to make notes or to sketch a writing plan on some rough paper before writing their answer. If a limit has been set, planning time should be counted within the given time frame.

Once your child has completed a task, talk through their writing and try to offer positive, constructive feedback. (Follow the links to *How To Do 11+ English* and *Focus on Comprehension* to find out more about the conventions and requirements of different writing styles.) As it can be difficult to mark a piece of writing, a suggested marking scheme for each task can be found on pages 14–15. 17/20 equals the target score of 85% (see 'The secrets of 11+ success in English' booklet). Some general guidelines for assessing writing have also been provided.

Answers and explanations

Test 1

Questions 1 to 25

1	D	The introduction states that Bronia (aged 3) is Ruth (aged 12) and Edek's (aged 11) younger sister.
2	A	The introduction states that the story is set in Poland.
3	B	The introduction states that the children 'are fleeing from the house across the roof after the storm troopers had dragged their mother away'.
4	B	Line 13 states that the children 'made their new home in a cellar at the other end of the city.'
5	A	Lines 4–7 describe the city being bombed. This would have resulted in buildings in the city being destroyed, becoming piles of rubble.
6	C	The passage suggests that many people were in a similar situation to the children (i.e. the destruction of their town; the number of people living in the wood; the number of children working as smugglers) so the most likely explanation is that the Polish Council of Protection was unable to know exactly where every missing person went.
7	E	Lines 29–30 state that Ruth and Bronia 'were allowed to draw the small rations' that the Nazis allowed.
8	D	Lines 33–34 state that Polish Welfare set up soup kitchens which provided food for people in need, like the children of the story.
9	D	As stated in line 36, the Nazis were the children's enemies and had caused the situation that led the children to be hungry and without their parents. As such, the children felt it was justified for them to steal the food.
10	D	Line 38–39 state that they slept under 'an oak tree which Edek had chosen for the shelter of its branches'. This suggests that Edek wanted to shelter the children from the weather.
11–12	B, E	**B:** The children living in the forest had nowhere to go all day, so by starting a school Ruth could keep them busy.
		E: It is also likely that the Nazis had closed the schools the children living in the woods normally attended.
13	B	Lines 47 and 48 state that the *Biedronka* was smuggled into the woods, which suggests that it had to be hidden from the Nazis. Also, it was published by the Polish Underground press: the term 'underground' is used here to mean a group that works secretly against a government. As it is likely that the Nazis would have seized a journal produced by an underground group, the *Biedronka* had to be kept secret.
14	C	Lines 49–50 state 'The grubby finger marks showed that other families had seen it before them.'
15–16	A, C	**A:** By controlling the food supply the Nazis could make sure that their soldiers were given enough food by giving them first choice.
		C: By controlling something people need in order to live, the Nazis were able to control the lives of the Polish citizens.
17	D	Lines 56–57 state that 'In return for his services, he was given all the food he needed for the family.'
18	D	Edek was nearly caught by the Nazis smuggling butter and eggs in the logs. Line 70 states that 'After that, Edek did all his smuggling at night', which suggests that he felt that he would have a lower risk of being spotted by the Nazis if he did the smuggling at night.
19	E	'Relieved' means free from worry or stress, which is how Edek would have felt when he escaped being caught by the Nazi police patrol. The other options are all words associated with being frightened or unsuccessful.
20	B	'Distraught' means to be very upset, which is how Ruth would have felt after learning that Edek had been captured. Neither 'concerned' nor 'frustrated' are strong enough words to express the feelings Ruth would have after such a devastating event.
21	D	Lines 61–62 describe what would happen if a boy Edek's age was caught: 'But boys as strong as he was would be carried off to Germany, for the Nazis

		were getting short of labour at home.' This suggests that Edek would have been taken to Germany and forced to work.
22	B	As demonstrated several times in the passage, the children are forced to take on the role of adults. They are responsible for finding shelter (lines 22–27) and food (lines 29–36) – activities which are usually the responsibilities of an adult.
23	C	The most devastating event for the children was not knowing where their parents were or what had happened to them. Therefore, the possibility of seeing them again would have been the main factor for the children wanting to survive. The other options would most likely have been less important reasons for wanting to survive.
24	A	These lines state that Edek provided food, clothes and money for his sisters as well as making sure that they were safe and warm.
25	C	The introduction states that the children's mother is arrested.

D 9

26	B	'Revealing' means 'making new or secret information known'. Lines 31–33 suggest that Edek wanted to keep his age a secret from the Nazis, and 'revealing' is closer in meaning to 'disclosing' than the other options.
27	D	A 'black market' is one in which goods are sold illegally. Lines 52–55 state that it was illegal for food to be sold to anyone other than the Nazis. As such, a market that sold food to Polish citizens would be illegal.
28	E	'Quail' means to 'feel or show fear'. This makes answer choice E the best option.
29	B	The phrase 'a heavy heart' means feeling sad, sorrowful or weary. This is the best option, as Ruth would feel great sadness after learning that Edek had been captured and knowing that she needed to tell Bronia.

D 6

30	D	These words are pronouns because they are used instead of a noun to indicate someone already mentioned or known.

C 4

31	B	Answer choice B is the only option that includes a comparison using the word 'like'.

D 6

32	C	Only answer choice C is a noun that refers to a feeling or a concept.

E 2

33	D	environment

E 2

34	A	circumstances

E 2

35	B	behaviour

E 2

36	D	incomprehensible

E 2

37	A	unnecessary

E 2

38	A	outrageous

D 5

39	B	An exclamation mark is missing after the word 'quick'. The sentence should read: "All right, but be quick! What do you want? Biscuits?" A full stop instead of an exclamation mark would also be correct.

D 5

40	D	An apostrophe is missing in the word 'its' because as used here it means 'it is'. The section of the sentence should read: Robin and Naomi refused to be hurried. "Chocolate biscuits are nice for tea but if it's for a pudding as well,

D 4

41	C	A comma is missing after the word 'good'. The section of the sentence should read: which it looks as if it might be, shortbread is good," said Naomi.

D 1

42	A	The 'w' in the first 'we' should be capitalized because it is beginning a new sentence. The section of the sentence should read: "We didn't have any supper last night," Robin explained…

43 C — A question mark is missing after the word 'biscuits' and is needed because it is the end of a sentence. The question should read: In case that happens again, Alex, don't you think we better stock up with biscuits?"

44 A — An apostrophe is missing in the word 'well' because it is a contraction of the words 'we will'. The section of the sentence should read: "All right, we'll take a packet of ginger, one of chocolate and the shortcake…".

45 B — 'Higher' is the correct option because the sentence is comparing two objects (the kites). 'Highest' would be correct if more than two kites were being compared. 'More higher' and 'most higher' are not proper terms. 'High' does not make sense in the sentence.

46 A — 'Did' is the correct option because it is the correct tense for the sentence. With the exception of 'done', which is the wrong tense, the other options are not proper words.

47 D — 'Who' is the correct option because the missing word must refer to 'my friend' and 'who' is a pronoun that refers to a person.

48 A — 'I' is the correct option because both people being discussed (cousin and I) are the subjects of the sentence (they are doing something).

49 B — 'We're' is the contraction of the words 'we are' and is the only option that makes sense in the sentence. The others all sound similar to 'we're' when spoken but don't make sense in the sentence: 'were' is a form of the verb 'be', 'weir' is a type of dam, 'wear' means to have clothing on one's body, and 'where' refers to a place or position.

50 B — 'Lying' is the correct option because it is the correct tense for the sentence and is also the correct option for an action that involves lying down on a flat surface.

Test 2

Questions 1 to 25

1 E — Line 4 states that 'The good news is that we have secured a dhow to take us to Bombay.'

2 E — In line 5, Michael Palin states that he will be taking a six-day voyage on an open boat. As he is retracing the voyage of Phileas Fogg, it is most likely that Phileas Fogg also took a boat to Bombay. Also, lines 6–7 state that 'Phileas Fogg, aboard the *Mongolia* all the way, reached Bombay in eighteen days.'

3–4 A, C — As they are no longer called dhows by the people who use them, it is likely that:
A: only people who have a wide vocabulary, such as people who enjoy crossword puzzles, would still use the term.
C: only people who enjoy looking to the past or who have a romantic idea of how dhows were used in the past would still use the term.

5 B — In describing a dhow Michael Palin states in lines 9–10 that 'They are wooden, built to a traditional design resembling in shape a slice of melon…'.

6 E — Line 16 states 'Every one of the dhows is… generally run by family and friends…'.

7 D — In discussing the dhows, Michael Palin states in line 17 that most dhows were owned by 'some shrewd import-exporter in a stretch Mercedes', which suggests that the owners are wealthy.

8 C — Lines 18–20 suggest that most docks today are different as they are used by large ships that carry many people or large amounts of goods: 'Instead of cranes and gantries and hard-hats and bulk loads and lorries, operating behind guardposts and fences, the dhows are serviced, right in the centre of town …'.

9	B	Lines 19–20 state that '… the dhows are serviced, right in the centre of town, by small pick-up trucks, trolleys…', which suggests that the area was too small for large ships to enter.
10	A	Lines 20–21 state 'People bustle around, scrambling over the boats like ants, arranging, moving, heaving and hoisting the cargo.' This suggests that, like ants, they were busy and focused on their tasks.
11–12	B, E	**B:** The size and build of the dhows suggest that they would have difficulty staying upright during heavy winds and high waves. **E:** It would be ineffective for the dhows to go out in a monsoon if their cargo were to get wet and ruined.
13	C	Lines 26–27 state '… bounds across the deckful of date sacks…'. Lines 44–45 state 'Osman being flat on his back against a sack of pistachio nuts…'.
14	B	Line 24 states 'In the afternoon we are taken by Kamis, an agent for the port and customs department…', which suggests that Kamis works for the Dubai government.
15	E	Lines 27–28, referring to Hassan Suleyman, state 'He smiles broadly and constantly, especially when giving us bad news, so it is a moment before it sinks in that he is telling us he will not be leaving tomorrow, but the next day…'. As Hassan Suleyman is smiling when he speaks, Michael Palin at first doesn't realise that he is being told bad news.
16	B	In line 34, the taxi driver says that the dhow is unclean. This suggests that his statement 'three days on a dhow, fifteen in hospital' means that although the trip may only take a few days, the dirty condition of the dhow will make Michael Palin sick and he will end up spending a great deal of time in hospital.
17	A	Line 29 states that the dhow will be leaving on Wednesday, 12 October. Working backwards, this means that the 10th must have been a Monday.
18	C	Lines 43–44, referring to the oil slick, state 'It extends for several miles, and is so obscene it silences us all.' The use of the word 'obscene' to describe the oil slick implies that it is deeply offensive and that they are bothered by it.
19	D	Line 44 states that the oil slick extends for several miles and it is most likely that it would take a dhow hours to pass through it as it is thick and the dhow would not be able to move very quickly.
20	C	In lines 50–51 Michael Palin states that 'An air of anti-climax hangs over the boat. The elation of the first few days has been replaced by impatience and now resignation.' This suggests that he is no longer excited and is instead quieter and more thoughtful.
21	E	Lines 55–56 state 'The clear bright skies are gone and it's cloudier, humid and very still.' This suggests that prior to this the sky was clear, making answer choice E, sunny, the best option.
22	A	Line 57 states 'Our seventh and last night on the dhow should be celebrated…', which suggests that the crew probably wanted to spend the last night on the dhow with Michael Palin and his team celebrating.
23	C	Lines 64–65 state '… we are opposite the port, but as the dhow cannot go alongside until customs and immigration have come aboard…'. This implies that before they can dock, the customs and immigration officials must check the goods and people on the dhow.
24	E	Lines 65–66, referring to lowering the anchor, state 'This procedure, like raising the sail, involves all hands – old men and boys, side by side, releasing the anchor…'. The most likely reason that all of the crew are needed to lower the anchor is that it is very heavy. None of the other answer options are stated or implied in the passage.
25	E	Line 72 states 'But I clutch a batch of addresses…'.
26	A	'Nostalgic' means longing for things, people or situations in the past. The word 'sentimental' is the closest answer option because one of its meanings is having feelings of sadness or tenderness for the past.
27	B	'Leaden' means dull, heavy or grey. This makes answer option B, 'dark and heavy-looking', the best option.

#	Ans	Explanation
28	C	'Elation' means being very happy or in high spirits. Only answer choice C, 'delight', is similar.
29	E	'Pervasive' means spread through all parts. Only answer choice E, 'widespread', is similar.
30	D	These words are adjectives because they are used to describe a noun. For example, the word 'humid' is used in line 56 to describe the weather.
31	B	A synonym for 'atmosphere' is ambience.
32	C	'On' is a preposition because it explains where Michael is going (on the boat).
33	A	desperately
34	D	experienced
35	B	orchestra
36	B	negative
37	D	thoroughly
38	C	favourite
39	A	A colon should be placed after the word 'me' because the first part of the sentence (she annoyed me) is then explained by the second part (I needed to be on my own for this). The sentence should read: She annoyed me: I needed to be on my own for this. A dash (–) or a full stop could also be used.
40	A	A question mark should be placed after the word 'something'. The sentence should read: "D'you want something?" I asked her.
41	A	An apostrophe should be placed in the word 'others' because it is a contraction of the words 'other is'. The sentence should read: "One's out and the other's in bed."
42	D	The first letter of the word 'Horsenose' should be capitalised because it is part of the name of the cottage.
43	C	An apostrophe should be placed in the word 'I'd' because it is a contraction of the words 'I had'.
44	D	A full stop should be placed after the word 'hills' because it is the end of a sentence. The sentences should read: The walls were covered with paintings of lakes and hills. I wondered…
45	C	'Eaten' is the correct option because it is the only proper word ('eated', 'ates' and 'ated' are not proper words) that is in the past tense.
46	D	'Written' is the correct option because it is the only proper word ('writed', 'wroted' and 'wroten' are not proper words) that is appropriate when used with the word 'have'.
47	C	'To' is the correct option because it is used to show direction. The word 'too' means 'also' and the word 'two' means the number 2. The others are not proper words.
48	B	'There's' is the correct option because it is a contraction of the words 'there is' and is the only option that makes sense in the sentence. The word 'their' means belonging to them so does not make sense when read in the sentence; 'they'res' is not a proper word; 'theres' is missing an apostrophe and without it is not a proper word; and the word 'theirs' does not make sense in this sentence.

49	A	'No one' is the only answer choice that makes sense when read in the sentence.
50	B	'Fewer' is used for comparing the number of things, for example, days off school.

Test 3

Questions 1 to 25

1	C	Lines 3–4 state '… the ground allowed to lie fallow, so that the low growth of the forest – thorn bushes, convolvulus and other tangles – had swept into the clearing and covered everything with a cloak'. This suggests that the land could not have been farmed recently because it was covered in wild plants.
2	E	The description of the undergrowth in lines 4–5 suggests that the vegetation was thick and covered everything. The comparison of the undergrowth with a web suggests that they have similar characteristics: a linking or joining of different strands.
3	C	Line 4 describes the type of plants that are growing in the forest: 'convolvulus and other tangles'. Lines 7–8 describe 'convolvulus-covered tree stumps'. Both references suggest that it is a vine-like plant.
4	D	Lines 8–9 state that 'robin-chats hopped perkily in search of grasshoppers, and looked startlingly like English robins'.
5	C	Line 12 states that the undergrowth was 'waist-high' and of the options, answer choice C, about 1 metre, is the only realistic option.
6	A	In line 15 Gerald Durrell states that he is hoping that the python has found some shade, which suggests that it is very hot. Also, an egg can only be fried if it is cooked, which suggests that the sun is hot enough to cook an egg.
7–8	B, E	**B:** Lines 17–18 state that Agustine's sarong was turning from 'scarlet to wine-red as it absorbed the sweat from his body'. **E:** Lines 18–19 state that his face was 'freckled with a mass of sweat-drops'.
9	B	The introduction states that Gerald was being assisted in his search for the python by some local hunters. Also, lines 30–31 state that 'The hunters had very thoughtfully set fire to all the grass in the vicinity, in an effort to smoke the reptile out.'
10–11	A, C	**A:** Lines 28–29 state that 'anything that lived in them would be in no danger of getting drowned in the rainy season'. **C:** Lines 29–30 state that 'The mouth of each cave was about eight feet across, and three feet high, which gave a snake, but not much else, room for manoeuvring.' This suggests that the entrance was small and narrow, which would help protect the snake from predators.
12	E	To 'worm' means to move by wriggling or crawling. 'Squirmed' also means wriggled.
13	E	Lines 36–37 state 'After the glare of the sunshine outside, the cave seemed twice as dark as it was…'.
14	D	Line 41 describes the python as 'shining in the torchlight as if freshly polished'. The python is also described as being 'about fifteen feet long… and fat. It was also in an extremely bad temper.' The last descriptions suggest that it was large and angry.
15	C	Lines 42–43 state that 'The longer the torch beam played on it the more prolonged and shrill did its hisses become, until they rose to an eerie shriek.'
16	B	In lines 46–49, Gerald is explaining how little room there is for him to turn around if the snake were to come down the cave after him, which suggests that he is concerned about the snake coming too near him. There is nothing in the passage that states or suggests that any of the other options were true.
17	E	Lines 60–61 state that the python had 'coiled itself into a tight knot, with the head lying in the centre of the coils, so when I had got the sapling into position I had to force the snake to show its head'. This suggests that the snake had curled itself into a coil and was hiding its head in an effort to protect itself.
18	D	Lines 76–77 state 'Wedged like a couple of outsize sardines in an undersized can we had no room to move except backwards…'. This suggests that they are jammed together in a space that is so small they have little room to move, making answer choice D the correct answer.

19	D	To be 'polished' is to be smooth and glossy. Answer choice D, shiny and smooth, is the closest in meaning.
20	C	Line 79 states that 'Bob laid hold of the sapling [the noose of which was around the snake's neck] and pulled at it grimly.' This reminded him of a blackbird tugging a worm from its hole.
21	C	Lines 83–84 state 'But, as he stepped back, he put his foot on a loose rock which twisted under him, and he fell flat on his back.'
22–23	A, D	**A:** Lines 88–89 state that Gerald and Bob could 'feel the rippling of the powerful muscles'. **D:** Line 90 states that 'the smooth scales slipped through our sweaty hands', which suggests that they were unable to hold onto the snake.
24	C	The large numbers of plants (lines 3–13), the variety of birds and insects (lines 6–11), and the hot temperature (lines 13–19) describe a jungle environment.
25	A	**A:** The phrase 'triumphant hiss' suggests that the python had won the battle with the men.
26	C	'Fallow' land is land that is left unseeded during a growing season, which makes answer choice C the best option.
27	B	'Undiminished' means not reduced or lessened. Answer choice B, 'no less', is the closest option.
28	E	'Momentary' means very brief, or lasting for only a moment. Answer choice E, 'temporary', is the closest option.
29	D	'Exhilarated' means happy, joyful or enlivened. Only answer choice D, 'concerned and anxious', does not have the same meaning as exhilarated.
30	C	'He' is a pronoun because it can be used instead of a noun to indicate someone already mentioned or known.
31	D	Answer choice D is the only option in which one thing is described as if it is something else without the use of the word 'like' or 'as'. In answer choice D, the tangles in the clearing are described as being a cloak.
32	B	'Agustine' is a proper noun because it is the name of a person.
33	C	machinery
34	C	innocence
35	B	impatient
36	B	official
37	B	accommodation
38	C	referred
39	D	The word 'when' should begin with a capital letter because it is the beginning of a sentence. The sentence should read: When the fifth blind man caught hold…
40	X	There are no errors in the sentence.
41	C	A full stop should be placed after the word 'shouted' because it is the end of a sentence. The sentence should read: Angry words were shouted.
42	D	The word 'some' should begin with a capital letter because it is the beginning of a sentence. The sentence should read: Some of them even began to laugh.
43	A	Speech marks should be placed after the question mark because it is the end of the direct speech. The sentence should read: "Why are you laughing?" enquired the King.
44	C	An apostrophe should be placed in the word 'elses' because it is showing belonging. The sentence should read: You are always quarrelling because you cannot see anyone else's point of view.

45 C 'They're' is the correct option because it is a contraction of the words 'they are' and is the only option that makes sense when read in the sentence.

46 A 'I' is the correct option because both people being discussed (you and I) are the subjects of the sentence (they are doing something).

47 E 'There were' is the correct option. 'There' is correct because it shows place or position whereas 'their' refers to ownership of something. 'Were' is correct because the subject of the sentence, the trees, is plural.

48 B 'Worst' is the correct word to use because the behaviour of many children is being compared. 'Baddest', 'worstest' and 'worsest' are not proper words. 'Worse' would be appropriate if only two things were being compared.

49 B 'Had done' is the correct option because it is the only one that fits the tense of the sentence. With the exception of 'done', which is the wrong tense, the other options are not proper phrases.

50 C 'Any' is correct because it is the only option that agrees with the idea behind the sentence that the survivors lacked water. Both 'no' and 'none' used after the words 'had not had' are double negatives and would, therefore, mean that the survivors did in fact have water.

Test 4

 Questions 1 to 25

1 C Line 1 states that he was born in 1929 so the correct answer is the 1920s.

2 E Lines 1–2 state that Martin Luther King Jr's father and grandfather were preachers, so it is likely that this had some influence on his choice to study religion. Also, the other people listed as answer choices played roles in Martin Luther King Jr's life *after* he had made his decision to study religion.

3 C Lines 5–8 state that Martin Luther King Jr. heard a lecture by Gandhi, read books about Gandhi and his ideas and 'eventually became convinced that the same methods could be employed by blacks to obtain civil rights in America'.

4 C Lines 5–11 describe how Martin Luther King Jr. thought that non-violent, or peaceful, methods would be an effective method for gaining equal rights for black Americans.

5 B Lines 16–18 and 21–22 show that after Rosa Parks was arrested for refusing to give up her seat on a bus, the Montgomery Bus Boycott began which involved thousands of people.

6 C Lines 17–18 state 'It was decided that black people in Montgomery would refuse to use the buses until passengers were completely integrated.'

7 D Line 21 states 'For thirteen months the 17,000 black people in Montgomery walked to work or obtained lifts…'.

8–9 C, E Lines 22–23 state that the 'loss of revenue and a decision by the Supreme Court forced the Montgomery Bus Company to accept integration…'.

10 A Lines 33–34 state '… a small group of black students read the book and decided to take action themselves. They started a student sit-in at the restaurant of their local Woolworth's…'.

11 D Lines 46–48 state that African Americans had 'considerable economic power. By selective buying, they could reward companies that were sympathetic to the civil rights movement while punishing those who still segregated their workforce.' The term 'selective buying' suggests that they should only buy from certain companies.

12 C Lines 52–54 explain that Martin Luther King Jr. believed that if black Americans voted, they could influence the results of elections. This suggests that government leaders supported by black Americans would then support civil rights.

13 B Lines 59–60 state 'However, during the first two years of his presidency, Kennedy failed to put forward his promised legislation.'

14–15 A, C A: Line 63 states that compared to a white child, a black child had 'about one-half as much chance of completing high school'.

	C:	Throughout the extract there are examples of racial discrimination, which shows that some employers would not hire someone who was black.
16	D	Lines 68–71 state that in an attempt to persuade Congress to pass the Civil Rights Bill, King and others persuaded people to participate in a protest meeting in Washington, D.C.
17	B	Line 72 states that King delivered his speech on 28th August so answer choice B – summer – is correct.
18	A	Lines 75–76 of King's *I have a dream* speech state that King wants the United States to uphold the idea 'that all men are created equal'.
19	D	In line 45, black Americans are referred to as African Americans. In line 77 King refers to black Americans as 'the sons of former slaves' and most slaves in the United States came from Africa.
20	D	Lines 82–83 state '… where they will not be judged by the colour of their skin but by the content of their character'.
21	E	Lines 103–104 state that he made his last speech on 3rd April 1968 and was assassinated the next day.
22	E	These lines show that in their attempts to gain equal rights, King and his followers risked being injured and jailed.
23	D	Repetition of the phrase, particularly because it is short and meaningful, would help the speech stay in people's minds and make it memorable.
24	D	Lines 101–102 state that he was given the Nobel Peace Prize.
25	C	It is a biography because it is a written account of another person's life.
26	A	'Injustice' means the quality of being unjust, unfair or wrong. This makes answer choice A, 'unfairness', the best option.
27	C	'Segregated' means separated or set apart from others.
28	E	A 'strategy' is a plan of action.
29	B	To 'participate' means to 'take part in'. Only answer choice B, 'stand back from', has a different meaning from to 'participate'.
30	B	'Red' is an adjective because it is used to describe a noun (hills).
31	C	Answer choice C is the only option in which one thing is described as if it is something else. In answer choice C, the state of Mississippi is being described as an oasis of freedom.
32	D	'But' is a connective because it joins parts of a sentence together.
33	D	campaign
34	C	eventually
35	A	particularly
36	D	achieve
37	A	marriage
38	A	assistant
39	B	Speech marks should be added before the word 'Oh' because it is the beginning of words spoken as dialogue. The sentence should read: Sid flew downstairs, and said, "Oh, Aunt Polly, come! Tom's dying."
40	D	An exclamation mark should be added after the word 'it' because it is the end of the sentence and Aunty Polly is expressing surprise. The sentence should read: "Rubbish! I don't believe it!"
41	B	A comma should come after 'nevertheless' because the next part of the sentence is a separate clause. The sentence should read: But she fled upstairs nevertheless, with Sid and Mary at her heels.

D1
42 A The word 'her' should begin with a capital letter because it is the beginning of a sentence. The sentence should read: 'Her lip trembled.'

D5
43 B A question mark should be added after the word 'child' because it is the end of a sentence. The sentence should read: "What's the matter with you, child?"

44 X There are no errors.

D6
45 A 'Did well' is the only option that uses the correct tense.

D6
46 A 'We' is the only option that uses the correct plural.

E2
47 B 'Whether' is used to introduce an alternative (would the rain stop or not). 'Wether' and 'wheather' are not proper words. 'Weather' refers to the climate and 'wetter' refers to something being wet.

D13
48 B 'More beautiful' is the correct option because the sentence is comparing two dolls. 'Most beautiful' would be correct if more than two dolls were being compared and 'beautifullest' is not a proper word. 'Beautiful' on its own also does not make sense in the sentence.

E2
49 A Of the three homophones, 'rein' is the correct spelling for the reference to the strap of a stirrup used on a horse. 'Rain' is precipitation and 'reign' is the rule of a king or queen. The remaining options are not proper words.

E2
50 B 'Inappropriate' is correct because it is the only option that is a proper word and that fits grammatically in the sentence. The others are either not proper words (unappropriate, nonappropriate), do not fit grammatically with the sentence (none appropriate) or have a meaning that does not fit with the sentence ('misappropriate' means to steal something you have been trusted to take care of).

General guidelines for answering writing tasks

The following guidelines give you a number of general points to check for and discuss with your child on completion of the writing tasks.

- Children are required to write unaided at reasonable length. They need to show that they can structure their ideas effectively whilst keeping in mind the audience they are writing for and the purpose of the writing, if required, conveying their feelings and opinions succinctly.

- Children need to use punctuation marks correctly and know where appropriate speech marks, colons, semi-colons, hyphens, and so on, should be used. Remember to check that they start a new line when introducing conversation in the text. A wide range of devices should be used to build cohesion within and across paragraphs.

- The grammar used should represent 'good practice', particularly encompassing an interesting and appropriate variety of verbs, adjectives, adverbs, pronouns, prepositions and conjunctions, together with descriptive and evocative phrases and clauses to enhance their work. Sentences should vary in length to add interest. Children need to demonstrate the difference between the correct use of potentially confusing words, such as *their*, *there* and *they're*. Using the correct form and tense of verbs is essential.

Writing Task A

Use the *General guidelines for answering writing tasks* and the marking scheme below to award a total of 20 possible marks.

- Up to 2 marks for beginning the text with an introduction that explains which side of the debate the writer is supporting.

- Up to 2 marks for having a clear structure with an introduction, a middle section and a conclusion.

- Up to 2 marks for finishing the text with a conclusion that summarises the issue and the writer's position.

- Up to 3 marks for including facts from, or reasoned thoughts based on, the extract that support the writer's point of view.

- Up to 3 marks for addressing the other side of the issue.

- 1 mark for dividing the text into paragraphs.

- 2 marks for linking points through the use of connective words or phrases such as 'however', 'on the other hand', 'in comparison'.

- 1 mark for writing within the word limit (up to 250 words).

- Up to 2 marks for correct grammar and punctuation (beginning a sentence with a capital letter, correct use of commas or full stops, etc.).

- Up to 2 marks for overall accurate spelling.

For more guidance on how to answer evaluation or debate questions, see *Focus on Comprehension*, Step 2: Introduce personal opinion, section C.

Writing Task B

Use the *General guidelines for answering writing tasks* and the marking scheme below to award a total of 20 possible marks.

- 1 mark for including the writer's name and the date on the right-hand side.

- 3 marks for including the recipient's name and address details (fictitious) on the left-hand side and for writing an appropriate form of address for the leader of a country (Dear Sir/Madam, Your Excellency, etc.) and closing (Respectfully, etc.) including signing the letter.

- 1 mark for writing in the present tense.

- Up to 2 marks for writing in a formal style.

- Up to 2 marks for writing in clear, well-structured paragraphs.

- Up to 4 marks for writing in the first person (as Michael Palin), explaining clearly who Michael Palin is and for giving clear information about his journey, using facts and evidence from the extract.

- Up to 2 marks for clearly explaining the purpose of and reasons for wanting to visit the country.

- 1 mark for writing within the word limit (up to 250 words).

- Up to 2 marks for correct grammar and punctuation (beginning a sentence with a capital letter, correct use of commas or full stops, etc.).

- Up to 2 marks for overall accurate spelling.

For more guidance on writing letters, see *How To Do 11+ English*, section C7 and *Focus on Comprehension*, Step 1: Recognise different text types, section G.

Writing Task C

Use the *General guidelines for answering writing tasks* and the marking scheme below to award a total of 20 possible marks.

- Up to 3 marks for writing a continuation that fits with the story (same setting, themes, etc.).

- 1 mark for writing in the first person from the perspective of Durrell, the narrator.

- 1 mark for writing in the past tense.

- Up to 2 marks for including references to events or people that occurred in the extract.

- Up to 5 marks for following the same engaging writing style as the extract, e.g. the use of evocative language for describing plants, animals and the environment, and for showing peaks of excitement.

- Up to 2 marks for following the same organization and structure as the extract regarding sentence and paragraph length and for using similar types of words.

- 1 mark for including dialogue, shown as direct speech with the use of speech marks.

- 1 mark for writing within the word limit (up to 250 words).

- Up to 2 marks for correct grammar and punctuation (beginning a sentence with a capital letter, correct use of speech marks for dialogue, etc.).

- Up to 2 marks for overall accurate spelling.

For more guidance on how to answer text continuation questions, see *Focus on Comprehension*, Step 2: Introduce personal opinion, section B.

Writing Task D

Use the *General guidelines for answering writing tasks* and the marking scheme below to award a total of 20 possible marks.

- Up to 2 marks for retelling the different parts of the event in the order in which they happened.

- 1 mark for writing in the past tense.

- Up to 2 marks for writing in well-structured paragraphs including an introduction and a conclusion.

- Up to 2 marks for linking points through the use of connective words or phrases, such as 'first, next, then, however, finally'.

- Up to 5 marks for writing a lively retelling, including details of:

    1 mark for explaining where and when the event took place

    Up to 2 marks for describing the type of audience (parents, friends, classmates, etc.)

    Up to 2 marks for explaining the aim or purpose of the event

- Up to 3 marks for explaining how the experience made them feel, including details.

- 1 mark for writing within the word limit (up to 250 words).

- Up to 2 marks for correct grammar and punctuation (beginning a sentence with a capital letter, correct use of commas or full stops, etc.).

- Up to 2 marks for overall accurate spelling.

For more guidance on how to write an account or report, see *How To Do 11+ English*, section C7 and *Focus on Comprehension*, step 1: Recognise different text types, section E.

11+ English

Multiple-choice Test Papers
Pack 1
Test 1

Read the following carefully:

- Do not begin the test or open this booklet until told to do so
- Work as quickly and as carefully as you can
- Answers should be marked in pencil in the answer booklet provided, not in this test booklet
- You may do rough working on a separate sheet of paper
- If you make a mistake rub out the mistake and write the new answer clearly
- Be careful to keep your place in the accompanying answer booklet
- You will have 50 minutes to complete the test plus 5 minutes to read the comprehension text

OXFORD
UNIVERSITY PRESS

Great Clarendon Street, Oxford, OX2 6DP, United Kingdom

Oxford University Press is a department of the University of Oxford. It furthers the University's objective of excellence in research, scholarship, and education by publishing worldwide. Oxford is a registered trade mark of Oxford University Press in the UK and in certain other countries

Text © Sarah Lindsay 2015
Illustrations © Oxford University Press 2015

The moral rights of the author have been asserted

First published in 2015

All rights reserved. No part of this publication may be reproduced, stored in a retrieval system, or transmitted, in any form or by any means, without the prior permission in writing of Oxford University Press, or as expressly permitted by law, by licence or under terms agreed with the appropriate reprographics rights organization. Enquiries concerning reproduction outside the scope of the above should be sent to the Rights Department, Oxford University Press, at the address above.

You must not circulate this work in any other form and you must impose this same condition on any acquirer

British Library Cataloguing in Publication Data
Data available

978-0-19-274083-0

Paper used in the production of this book is a natural, recyclable product made from wood grown in sustainable forests. The manufacturing process conforms to the environmental regulations of the country of origin.

Printed in China

Acknowledgements

The publishers would like to thank the following for permissions to use copyright material:

The Silver Sword by Ian Serrailler, published by Jonathan Cape. Reprinted by permission of The Random House Group Ltd
The Growing Summer by Noel Streatfield (Copyright © Noel Streatfield)

Cover illustrations: Lo Cole

Although we have made every effort to trace and contact all copyright holders before publication this has not been possible in all cases. If notified, the publisher will rectify any errors or omissions at the earliest opportunity.

Links to third party websites are provided by Oxford in good faith and for information only. Oxford disclaims any responsibility for the materials contained in any third party website referenced in this work.

Read the extract carefully, then answer the questions in the answer booklet provided.

'The Silver Sword' by Ian Serraillier describes the plight of Ruth (12), Edek (11) and Bronia (3) who lived in Poland during the Second World War. These three children learnt what it really meant to survive after their father and mother were taken from them by the Nazis. The extract starts as they are fleeing from the house across the roof after the storm troopers had dragged their mother away and bundled her into a van, after locking the children in the house.

Luckily for them all the houses on this side of the road together were in one long terrace, otherwise they could not have got away. Even so, it was a miracle that none of their slips and tumbles ended in disaster.

They must have gone fully a hundred yards when the first explosion shook the air. A sheet of fire leapt up from their home into the frosty night sky. They fell flat in the snow and lay there. The roof shook, the whole city seemed to tremble. Another explosion. Smoke and flames poured from the windows. Sparks showered into the darkness.

'Come along,' said Edek. 'We shan't let them have us now.'

With growing confidence they hurried along the rooftops. At last, by descending a twisted fire escape, they reached street level. On and on they hurried, not knowing or caring where they went so long as they left those roaring flames behind them.

They did not stop till the fire was far away and the pale winter dawn was breaking.

They made their new home in a cellar at the other end of the city. They had tunnelled their way into it. From the street it looked like a rabbit's burrow in a mound of rubble, with part of a wall rising behind. On the far side there was a hole in the lower part of the wall, and this let in light and air as well as rain.

When they asked the Polish Council of Protection about their mother, they were told she had been taken off to Germany to work on the land. Nobody could say which part of Germany. Though they went many times to ask, they never found out any more. 'The war will end soon,' they were told. 'Be patient, and your mother will come back.'

But the war dragged on, and their patience was to be sorely tried.

They quickly made their new home as comfortable as they could. Edek, who could climb like a monkey, scaled three storeys of a bombed building to fetch a mattress and some curtains. The mattress he gave to Ruth and Bronia. The curtains made good sheets. On wet days they could be used over the hole in the wall to keep the rain out. With floorboards he made two beds, chairs, and a table. With bricks from the rubble he built a wall to divide the cellar into two rooms, one to live in and one to sleep in. He stole blankets from a Nazi supply dump, one for each of them.

Here they lived for the rest of that winter and the following spring.

Food was not easy to find. Ruth and Bronia had green Polish ration cards and were allowed to draw the small rations that the Nazis allowed. But, except when Edek found casual work, they had no money to buy food. Edek had no ration card. He had not dared to apply for one, as that would have meant disclosing his age. Everyone over twelve had to register, and he would almost certainly have been carried off to Germany as a slave worker. Whenever possible they ate at the soup kitchens which Polish Welfare had set up. Sometimes they begged at a nearby convent. Sometimes they stole from the Nazis or scrounged from their garbage bins. They saw nothing wrong in stealing from their enemies, but they were careful never to steal from their own people …

In the early summer they left the city and went to live in the woods outside. It was cold at night out in the open. They slept huddled together in their blankets under an oak tree which Edek had chosen for the shelter of its branches. There was not much rain that summer, though they had one or two drenchings in May. After that Edek cut down some branches, lashed them together and made a lean-to. This was thick enough to keep out all but the heaviest rain.

Life was much healthier here than in the city. The sun browned their limbs. There were plenty of other families to play with, some of them Jews who had escaped from the Warsaw ghetto. They could run about freely and hold their classes under the trees, without having to keep a look-out for police patrols. Ruth had started a school. Sometimes she had as many as twenty-five children there. She would have taken more, but they had no paper, very few slates, and no books at all.

Occasionally they received a smuggled copy of a secret journal specially published for children by the Polish Underground press. It was called *Biedronka*, 'The Ladybird', and was full of the kind of stories and pictures and jokes that children enjoy. The grubby finger marks showed that other families had seen it before them. When Ruth's children had finished with it, there was nothing left but a few tattered strips.

Because of the kindness of the peasants, food was more plentiful. Though they were forbidden to store food or to sell it to anyone but the Nazis, they gave the children whatever they could spare. They hid it, too, in cellars, in haystacks, in holes in the ground. With the help of the older children they smuggled it to the towns and sold it to the Poles on the black market.

Edek was one of the chief smugglers. In return for his services, he was given all the food he needed for the family. One of his dodges was to go off to town with pats of butter sewn into the lining of his coat. But he could only do this on cool days or at night. On hot days the butter melted. So he preferred to work at night if he could. In time the Germans became wary and posted patrols on all the main roads into the city. After that he cut across country, using paths and rough tracks. He was well aware of the penalties if he was caught. A younger child might get away with a beating. But boys as strong as he was would be carried off to Germany, for the Nazis were getting short of labour at home.

Another of Edek's dodges was the cartload of logs which he drove into the suburbs.

Some of the logs were split, their centres scraped out and packed with butter and eggs, then glued together again. Once he drove his cartload into a police patrol, which was searching everything on the road. They emptied the logs on to the pavement. Edek didn't stay to see if the glue would stand up to that treatment. He dived into the crowd and made off. Police whistles were blowing and the chase had started, when some kind friend lifted him up and pitched him head first into a garbage cart. Here he lay hidden, under cinders and dust and rotting vegetables.

After that, Edek did all his smuggling at night.

There came a morning, towards the end of August, when he failed to return. Ruth questioned other families in the forest, but no one had seen him. After some days of searching, she traced him to a village ten miles away. Edek had called at a house there while the secret police were searching for hidden stores. They had found cheese sewn into the lining of his coat. After setting fire to the house, they had taken him away in the van, with the house owner as well.

Ruth returned to the forest with a heavy heart, dreading to break the news to Bronia.

Edek had been their life-line. Food, clothes, money – they depended on him for all these. In the city he had made a home out of a ruin. In the woods no tree gave better shelter than the oak he had chosen. And after dark, when the wind blew cold and the damp oozed out of the ground, none knew better than he how to keep the fire in untended till dawn, so that the glow from the embers should warm them all night as they slept.

Now Ruth and Bronia must fend for themselves. It was an ordeal before which the bravest spirit might quail.

From *The Silver Sword* by Ian Serraillier

1   Who was Bronia?

   A   Edek's friend
   B   A German guard
   C   Edek's older sister
   D   Edek's younger sister
   E   Ruth and Edek's mother

2   In which country is this extract from the story set?

   A   Poland
   B   Switzerland
   C   Germany
   D   Great Britain
   E   Austria

3 How did the children get away from the storm troopers?

   A by running into the cellar
   B by climbing across the roofs of buildings
   C by hiding in a garden
   D by disguising themselves as peasants
   E by mingling with the crowd of onlookers

4 Where did the children make their first home?

   A in a park
   B in a cellar
   C on the roof of a building
   D in a friend's house
   E in an old sports pavilion

5 Why did their new home look 'like a rabbit's burrow in a mound of rubble' (line 14)?

   A It was in a building that had been damaged by bombs.
   B It was in a building that had been ruined during a storm.
   C It was in a building that had decayed over time and collapsed.
   D The children had tried to disguise it so they wouldn't be found.
   E The children tried to make it cosy like a burrow to help them stay warm.

6 What is the most likely reason for the Polish Council of Protection not giving the children more information about where their mother was?

   A They only gave information to adults.
   B The children couldn't afford the fee they charged for providing information.
   C With so many people missing they couldn't be sure where she was.
   D They had other more important things to do and didn't have the time to help the children.
   E The children were from a different city so they couldn't help them.

7 Why were the ration cards the children had been issued of little use to them?

   A They were out of date.
   B They could only be used if their mother was with them.
   C They only allowed the children to have food that they didn't know how to cook.
   D They could only be used in shops that were in another city.
   E They allowed them only very limited amounts of food.

8 Based on the information in the extract, what was the role of Polish Welfare (line 34)?

   A To help people who wanted to move to Germany.
   B To raise money to help start rebuilding cities destroyed in the war.
   C To help the Nazi government make sure Polish citizens followed their laws.
   D To help Polish citizens who were in need as a result of the Nazis' actions.
   E To keep track of Polish citizens who were missing.

9 Why do you think the children saw 'nothing wrong' in stealing from the Nazis?

   A They knew the Nazis didn't like Polish food anyway.
   B They didn't think that the Nazis would really mind.
   C They thought that the Nazis would give them the food eventually anyway.
   D They felt it was acceptable because the Nazis were the people who had caused them to go hungry and be without their parents.
   E They believed that the food would just be wasted if they didn't take it.

10 What made Edek choose the tree he did for the children to sleep under?

   A It was on a hill.
   B It was close to water.
   C It was away from other people.
   D It provided protection from the weather.
   E It was close to the paths they used to go into town.

Continue to the next page

11–12 Choose the two most probable reasons for Ruth deciding to start a school.
  A She wanted to earn money.
  B It would help to occupy the younger children during the day.
  C She wanted to keep the children away from the busy streets.
  D She had been asked by the Nazi government to start the school.
  E The schools the children normally attended had been closed because of the war.

13 Why did the *Biedronka* need to be a 'secret journal' (line 47)?
  A Ruth knew that it had been stolen.
  B The Nazis had not given their permission for it to be published.
  C The adults did not like the children reading it and would have taken it away.
  D It contained secret information about what was happening in the war.
  E It was only meant to be read by adults.

14 How did Ruth know that others had already read *Biedronka*?
  A It had been sent with a letter from someone explaining how much they had enjoyed it.
  B All of the pictures had been coloured and the puzzles filled in.
  C The pages were dirty where people had handled it.
  D The names of people who had read it were written on the cover.
  E A bookmark was left in it.

15–16 Choose the two most likely reasons for the Nazis wanting to control the food supply.
  A Their first priority was to feed their soldiers, which they could do if they controlled the food supply.
  B They wanted people to become used to eating German food.
  C They wanted the local people to be reminded that the Nazis were now in control of their lives.
  D They thought that it would be difficult for the Polish people to get food without their help.
  E They wanted to help the Polish farmers who they believed were not earning enough money.

17 According to the extract, what is the *main* reason Edek became a smuggler?
  A He liked the excitement of trying to trick the Nazis.
  B It gave him an opportunity to meet people now that he was away from his home and friends.
  C He thought that he might meet people who would help him find his mother.
  D It allowed him to provide for himself and his sisters.
  E It allowed him to get some work experience so he could later find a better job.

18 Why did Edek prefer to smuggle at night (line 70)?
  A The people who received the smuggled goods were at work in the day so it was easier for Edek to contact them at night.
  B All of the boys who were new at smuggling were forced to do so at night.
  C There were more people out at night so he had a better chance of blending into a crowd.
  D It was harder for the Nazi soldiers to spot him during the night.
  E It allowed him to help Ruth teach the children during the day.

19 Which of these words do you think best describes how Edek felt when he escaped being caught by the police patrol (lines 65–70)?
  A unlucky
  B anxious
  C alarmed
  D scared
  E relieved

20 Which of these words best describes Ruth's mood on finding out what happened to Edek (line 76)?
  A frustrated
  B distraught
  C concerned
  D thoughtful
  E courageous

Please turn over

21 What probably happened to Edek after he was captured?
  A He joined the Polish army.
  B He became a Nazi soldier.
  C He ran away to try to find his mother.
  D He was taken to Germany and forced to work for the Nazis.
  E He was taken and placed in a school for children who had lost their parents.

22 What best describes the effect the experiences detailed in the extract have on the children?
  A They learn about different ways of living and make new friends.
  B They have to take on responsibilities that are usually handled by adults.
  C They enjoy their time without having their parents around because they are able to do what they want.
  D They enjoy not having to go to school.
  E They are able to live in, and learn about, different parts of their town.

23 What would have made the children most determined to survive the Nazi occupation of Poland?
  A The desire to read any journal or book they wanted.
  B The prospect of having new clothes again.
  C The hope of being reunited with their parents.
  D The thought of not having to use ration books again.
  E The anger that their home was bombed and they were forced to flee.

24 Based on the information in lines 77–81, which of these statements about Edek is true?
  A He provided for his sisters' basic needs so they would survive.
  B He relied on his sisters to take care of themselves.
  C He was frightened and wanted to go to the Nazis for help.
  D He spent most of his time trying to find their mother.
  E He left his sisters on their own while he tried to find someone to help them.

25 Which event occurred first?
  A Edek is arrested for smuggling cheese.
  B Ruth starts teaching local children.
  C Mother is arrested by storm troopers.
  D They build a shelter in a cellar.
  E They live in the woods.

Answer these questions about the meanings of words or phrases as they are used in the extract.

26 What is the closest meaning to 'disclosing' (line 32)?
  A announcing
  B revealing
  C uttering
  D registering
  E writing

27 What is meant by the 'black market' (line 55)?
  A a free market
  B an expensive market
  C a market that happens at night
  D an illegal market
  E a market run by the Nazi government

28 What is the closest definition to the word 'quail' (line 83)?
  A to be rewarded
  B to look forward to
  C to prepare for
  D to run from
  E to show fear

29 What is meant by 'a heavy heart' (line 76)?

Continue to the next page

A a feeling of relief
B great sadness
C joyfulness
D feeling frightened
E feeling confused

Answer the following questions about these words and phrases.

30 What class of words are these?

themselves   him   they   she

A adjectives
B common nouns
C verbs
D pronouns
E adverbs

31 Which of these lines from the extract includes a simile?
A In the early summer they left the city
B Edek, who could climb like a monkey
C Sometimes they begged at a nearby convent
D the Germans became wary and posted patrols
E He dived into the crowd

32 Which of these words from the extract is an abstract noun?
But the war dragged on, and their patience was to be sorely tried.
     A   B C   D E

In these sentences there are a number of spelling mistakes. Choose the letter where the spelling mistake is underlined or, if there isn't a spelling mistake, choose the letter X.

33 Although they were determined to withstand the terrible deprivations,
     A   B
they longed for a more comfortable enviroment.
     C   D   X

34 Under no circumstanses would the Germans permit
     A   B
the trading of foodstuffs by the peasant population.
     C   D   X

35 Little did she realise the invaders' behavour was going to be the catalyst
     A   B   C
for so many tragic events.
     D   X

36 There was to be a catalogue of disasters on a scale that in normal times
     A   B   C
would have been considered incomprehensable.
     D   X

37 It is totally unecessary for invading soldiers to be as cruel and vindictive
     A   B   C
as the Nazis were throughout the war.
     D   X

38 The outragous attitude of the Nazis during the war was to haunt fair-minded Germans
     A   B   C
for generations to come.
     D   X

Please turn over

In this extract, mistakes have been made in the use of punctuation and capital letters. In your answer booklet, mark the letter where the mistake is underlined. If there isn't a mistake, mark the letter X.

Alex wanted nothing except to get Robin and Naomi out of the shop.

39 "All right, but be quick What do you want? Biscuits?"
    A   B   C   D   X

40 Robin and Naomi refused to be hurried. "Chocolate biscuits are nice for tea but
    A   B   C

if its for a pudding as well,
   D   X

41 which it looks as if it might be, shortbread is good" said Naomi.
    A   B   C   D   X

42 "we didn't have any supper last night," Robin explained to the company,
    A   B   C

"because we were all too scared to go to the kitchen.
   D   X

43 In case that happens again, Alex, don't you think we better stock up with biscuits"
    A   B   C

Alex would have agreed to almost anything.
   D   X

44 "All right, well take a packet of ginger, one of chocolate and the shortcake and those
    A   B   C

chocolates and sweets."
   D   X

From *The Growing Summer* by Noel Streatfeild

In this extract, choose the letter below the word or words that need to be chosen for the extract to make sense and use correct English.

45 Whose kite flies high higher highest more higher most higher, yours or mine?
                                       A   B   C   D   E

46 The children did had did done have did did done their best to keep warm.
                                A B   C   D   E

47 My friend which that whose who what lives next door plays very loud music.
                         A   B   C   D   E

48 My cousin and I me us we us both are going to Spain on holiday.
                           A B C D E

49 Sometime soon were we're weir wear where going to have lunch.
                        A   B   C   D   E

50 The rabbit was laying lying laid lain lied very still under the shed.
                      A   B   C   D   E

11+ English

Multiple-choice Test Papers
Pack 1
Test 2

Read the following carefully:

- Do not begin the test or open this booklet until told to do so
- Work as quickly and as carefully as you can
- Answers should be marked in pencil in the answer booklet provided, not in this test booklet
- You may do rough working on a separate sheet of paper
- If you make a mistake rub out the mistake and write the new answer clearly
- Be careful to keep your place in the accompanying answer booklet
- You will have 50 minutes to complete the test plus 5 minutes to read the comprehension text

OXFORD
UNIVERSITY PRESS

Great Clarendon Street, Oxford, OX2 6DP, United Kingdom

Oxford University Press is a department of the University of Oxford. It furthers the University's objective of excellence in research, scholarship, and education by publishing worldwide. Oxford is a registered trade mark of Oxford University Press in the UK and in certain other countries

Text © Sarah Lindsay 2015
Illustrations © Oxford University Press 2015

The moral rights of the author have been asserted

First published in 2015

All rights reserved. No part of this publication may be reproduced, stored in a retrieval system, or transmitted, in any form or by any means, without the prior permission in writing of Oxford University Press, or as expressly permitted by law, by licence or under terms agreed with the appropriate reprographics rights organization. Enquiries concerning reproduction outside the scope of the above should be sent to the Rights Department, Oxford University Press, at the address above.

You must not circulate this work in any other form and you must impose this same condition on any acquirer

British Library Cataloguing in Publication Data
Data available

978-0-19-274083-0

Paper used in the production of this book is a natural, recyclable product made from wood grown in sustainable forests. The manufacturing process conforms to the environmental regulations of the country of origin.

Printed in China

Acknowledgements

The publishers would like to thank the following for permissions to use copyright material:

Around the World in 80 Days by Michael Palin, published by BBC Books. Reprinted by permission of The Random House Group Ltd
The Snake-Stone by Bertie Doherty, Hamish Hamilton 1995 © Bertie Doherty 1995

Cover illustrations: Lo Cole

Although we have made every effort to trace and contact all copyright holders before publication this has not been possible in all cases. If notified, the publisher will rectify any errors or omissions at the earliest opportunity.

Links to third party websites are provided by Oxford in good faith and for information only. Oxford disclaims any responsibility for the materials contained in any third party website referenced in this work.

Read the extract carefully, then answer the questions in the answer booklet provided.

For a television programme, 'Around the World in 80 Days', Michael Palin with a film crew attempted to retrace the route Phileas Fogg had taken 115 years earlier. The following are some extracts from Michael Palin's diary.

Day 16
10 October

Woken from a five-hour sleep by the sound of a telephone at my bedside. Good news and bad news. The good news is that we have secured a dhow to take us to Bombay. The bad news is that it leaves at dawn tomorrow. No time for recovery before a six-day voyage on an open boat. On the other hand the sooner we move on the better. I must not forget that Phileas Fogg, aboard the *Mongolia* all the way, reached Bombay in eighteen days.

Walk out onto the quayside. My first sight of a dhow. Only nostalgic, crossword-loving Western romantics still call them dhows. To the locals they are 'launches' or 'coastal vessels'. They are wooden, built to a traditional design resembling in shape a slice of melon, with a high stern on which sits the wheelhouse, a draught of 15 or 20 feet, and a length of about 60 feet. There seems to be no shortage of them in Dubai. There are twenty or thirty lined up in this inlet of the river they call The Creek. One is loading crates of 'Tiger's Head' brand flashlights, made in China, 'Coast' full-cream milk powder, boxes of Tide washing powder, 'White Elephant' dry battery cells, Sanyo radios and a twin-tub washing machine. Its destination is Berbera in Somalia.

Every one of the dhows is like a floating small business, and generally run by family and friends, though owned, as likely as not, by some shrewd import–exporter in a stretch Mercedes. They present quite a different dockside ambience from any I've experienced so far. Instead of cranes and gantries and hard-hats and bulk loads and lorries, operating behind guardposts and fences, the dhows are serviced, right in the centre of town, by small pick-up trucks, trolleys and men's backs. People bustle around, scrambling over the boats like ants, arranging, moving, heaving and hoisting the cargo. The reason for the great activity at the moment is that these are some of the first boats out after the monsoon season from May to August, during which the dhows are laid up because of storms.

In the afternoon we are taken by Kamis, an agent for the port and customs department, to see the boat that will be our home for the next week. The M.V. *Al Sharma* (meaning 'Candlelight') is a trim, freshly-painted ship, and her Captain, Hassan Suleyman, bounds across the deckful of date sacks to welcome us. He smiles broadly and constantly, especially when giving us bad news, so it is a moment before it sinks in that he is telling us he will not be leaving tomorrow, but the next day, Wednesday, 12 October. Day 18.

All the time made up on the hectic scramble from Jeddah is suddenly lost again, but there is nothing we can do. Clem disappears to have words with the owners, Nigel and the other Passepartouts [the film crew] to the other end of the quay to film. I'm left with the taxi drivers. One nods towards the *Al Sharma*. 'You go on that?' He clearly can't believe it. The other joins in. 'These boats no restaurant!' He shakes his head vigorously, mistaking my smile for disbelief. 'No clean, nowhere sleep!' Now they both shake their heads, like witches. 'It will be six, seven days, you know. Terrible... Terrible! Three days on a dhow, fifteen in hospital!'

Day 19
13 October

All is pretty quiet aboard the *Al Sharma* this morning, the crew lie curled up on various parts of the deck, sleeping off the night's activity. Al Mamoun of course, is awake, already making chapatis and brewing tea. A small rattan mat of many colours is produced for us, and our breakfast of omelette, chapati, jam and fresh oranges laid out on it.

As we're eating the sea around us turns leaden and heavy. We're passing through the thick, viscous smear of an oil slick. It extends for several miles, and is so obscene it silences us all. Osman being flat on his back against a sack of pistachio nuts, Mahomet has taken his role as our guardian. Mahomet, wafer-thin and with a crop of curly black hair, is the father of Anwar, the cabin boy, and brother of the captain. He speaks more English than most because he worked for a while as an international seaman.

Day 24
18 October

   An air of anti-climax hangs over the boat. The elation of the first few days has been replaced by impatience and now resignation. At one time on the dhow I wanted time to stand still; now that it is, I just feel frustrated.

   Our speed has been cut to 4 knots, a pervasive odour of fish hangs over the boat, for most of yesterday's catch is being dried for the return voyage.... As I'm not eating I feel my energy reserves dwindling. Nowhere on the boat is comfortable any more. The clear bright skies are gone and it's cloudier, humid and very still. Even the weather seems to be waiting for something to happen.

   Our seventh and last night on the dhow should be celebrated but, as the *Al Sharma* turns in endless circles, wasting time, Passepartout [the film crew] and I are subdued and quite soon get our heads down, taking refuge in the world of personal stereo whilst the crew sit round in groups, talking, for most of the night. There's an end of term feeling aboard, and I feel that our inertia must be something of a disappointment to them.

Day 25
19 October

   At about 10 o'clock we are opposite the port, but as the dhow cannot go alongside until customs and immigration have come aboard, the crew prepare to weigh anchor. This procedure, like raising the sail, involves all hands – old men and boys, side by side, releasing the anchor and lowering it into the murky water. Scavenging crows board the ship, followed by three well-built customs men in dark glasses.

   So the time comes to say goodbye to the people in whose hands we have entrusted our lives for the last week. It's been a unique relationship, for I can't imagine any other circumstances in which we would have become so close so quickly to people like this, and of course it's hard to come to terms with the fact that it must end so peremptorily. But I clutch a batch of addresses and Kasim clutches me and I climb down the rope ladder to waves and smiles and 'Goodbye Mi-kels!' Then my launch speeds me to the quayside and I know I shall never see them again and I shall miss them.

From *Around the World in 80 Days* by Michael Palin

1 Where was Michael Palin planning to go in a dhow?

   A Somalia
   B China
   C Berbera
   D Dubai
   E Bombay

2 How did Phileas Fogg spend the first 18 days of his expedition travelling?

   A by train
   B on foot
   C by car
   D by plane
   E by boat

3–4 Choose two answers that explain why Michael Palin suggests that 'Only nostalgic, crossword-loving Western romantics still call them dhows'.

   A It is the type of old-fashioned or unusual word that typically appears in crossword puzzles.
   B Only people from Western countries are familiar with dhows.
   C Some people have old-fashioned images of dhows gently gliding through sunny, still seas instead of how they are actually used.
   D Dhow is a term that Western countries gave to the boats and was never used by local people.
   E Dhow is the English name for that type of boat.

Please turn over

5 What reminded Michael Palin of a slice of melon?
  A the inlet of the river
  B the shape of a dhow
  C a picture on the boxes of washing powder
  D the shape of the moon
  E the men's backs while servicing the dhows

6 Who usually worked on the dhows?
  1 importers 2 family 3 exporters 4 friends
  A 1 and 2
  B 2 and 3
  C 3 and 4
  D 1 and 3
  E 2 and 4

7 Who, does it seem, makes most money from the dhows?
  A the captains
  B the sailors
  C the customs officers
  D the owners
  E the passengers

8 Why does Michael Palin say he is unfamiliar with docks like the one in Dubai?
  A In most parts of the world only people who have been given permission can see such docks.
  B It is the only place in the world with this type of dock.
  C Most of the docks around the world now look different as they service only large ships.
  D He usually travels by plane so rarely sees docks.
  E There are no docks in Britain.

9 Why is it unlikely that large cargo vessels would have been tied up at the same quay as the dhows?
  A They failed to book a space early enough.
  B The area was too restricted for large boats to enter.
  C The dhow captains refused them permission.
  D The quays were allowed to take only one type of ship.
  E The dhows had taken all the berths.

10 Which answer best explains why Michael Palin likens people to ants (line 21)?
  A They were busy and purposeful in the work they were doing.
  B They moved very quickly as they worked.
  C From where he was standing they looked small.
  D They all wore the same dark uniforms.
  E They worked in long, orderly lines.

11–12 Choose two reasons that best explain why dhows tend not to go to sea during the annual monsoon.
  A The owners of the dhows only want them used a few times a year.
  B They are vulnerable in the strong winds and high waves.
  C The crews want to have their holidays during the dry weather.
  D The sea is too crowded with other ships.
  E The rain might damage the goods they carry on the deck.

13 What cargo is the *Al Sharma* carrying?
  A dates and radios
  B tea and oranges
  C pistachio nuts and dates
  D washing powder and milk powder
  E radios and flashlights

Continue to the next page

14 Who is Kamis?

  A a friend of the film crew
  B a government worker
  C a taxi driver
  D a relative of the captain
  E a sailor on the dhow

15 Why did the bad news from Hassan Suleyman take a few moments to sink in?

  A Michael wasn't concentrating on what he was being told.
  B Michael was admiring the freshly-painted *Al Sharma*.
  C Hassan didn't speak clearly.
  D Michael was worried Hassan was going to fall overboard.
  E Hassan's smile gave the impression nothing was wrong.

16 What does the taxi driver probably mean by 'three days on a dhow, fifteen in hospital'?

  A In three days aboard the dhow you will be hungry from a lack of food.
  B The conditions on the dhow are so unclean you will contract an illness.
  C It would be more comfortable spending time in hospital than it would be on the dhow.
  D It would be safer to travel by taxi.
  E Dhows are sometimes used as water ambulances.

17 What day of the week is the 10th of October?

  A Monday
  B Wednesday
  C Friday
  D Saturday
  E Sunday

18 Why does the oil slick silence everyone on the dhow?

  A They have never seen one before and are silent as they watch.
  B They believe that it looks beautiful and enjoy watching it in silence.
  C They realise the harmful effect it will have on the environment.
  D The captain is having a difficult time sailing through the oil slick so they remain quiet so as to not disturb him.
  E The loud noise the dhow makes passing through the oil slick makes it too difficult to hear one another so they remain silent.

19 How long would you expect it might have taken the *Al Sharma* to sail through the oil slick?

  A a few seconds
  B a few minutes
  C a few days
  D a few hours
  E a week

20 What word best describes how Michael Palin is feeling on Day 24?

  A chilly
  B excited
  C quiet
  D comfortable
  E elated

21 What best describes the weather for the first few days of the journey?

  A cloudy
  B humid
  C thundery
  D rainy
  E sunny

Please turn over

22 Why do you think the ship's crew might be disappointed that Michael Palin and his film crew went to bed early on the seventh night?

A They knew it was the last night they could enjoy their company.
B They had many questions they wanted to ask them.
C They needed to clean the area where their beds were.
D They wanted to play loud music.
E They wanted Michael Palin and the crew to help them work the dhow through the night.

23 Why can't the *Al Sharma* dock as soon as she arrives at the port?

A They are too early.
B They forgot to book a space.
C They have to have their cargo and personal papers checked.
D The waves are too big.
E They have to pay an entrance fee.

24 How do we know the anchor is heavy?

A Michael Palin states how much it weighs.
B It is made of iron which makes it very heavy.
C Michael Palin tries to lift it but can't.
D Michael Palin states that it looks heavy.
E The crew all need to work together to raise or lower it.

25 What indication is there that Michael Palin grew close to the crew of the *Al Sharma*?

A He asks them to meet him later during his journey.
B He asks them to visit him in England.
C They give him presents as he leaves the ship.
D They ask him to remain on the ship and travel back with them.
E He has collected their addresses so he can keep in contact.

Answer these questions about the meanings of words or phrases as they are used in the extract.

26 What is the closest definition to the word 'nostalgic' (line 8)?

A sentimental
B old
C thoughtful
D tired
E imaginative

27 What does it mean when the sea is described as being 'leaden' (line 43)?

A clear and calm
B dark and heavy-looking
C choppy
D smelly
E rough

28 What is the closest meaning to 'elation' (line 50)?

A relief
B trauma
C delight
D dejection
E tiredness

Continue to the next page

29 What is the closest meaning to 'pervasive' (line 53)?

- A sour
- B sweet
- C perfumed
- D unpleasant
- E widespread

Answer the following questions about these words and phrases.

30 The following are what type of words?

humid   small   murky   cracked

- A nouns
- B verbs
- C adverbs
- D adjectives
- E pronouns

31 Which of these lines from the extract includes a synonym for the word 'atmosphere'?

- A crossword-loving Western romantics
- B quite a different dockside ambience
- C the thick, viscous smear of an oil slick
- D People bustle around, scrambling over the boat like ants
- E I feel my energy reserves dwindling

32 Which of these words from the extract is a preposition?

"You go on that?" He clearly can't believe it.
A   B C   D   E

In these sentences there are a number of spelling mistakes. Choose the letter where the spelling mistake is underlined or, if there isn't a spelling mistake, choose the letter X.

33 She was desparately disturbed by the horrible conditions they had to endure.
    A   B   C   D   X

34 During the summer the temperatures climbed to levels they had not experinced hitherto.
    A   B   C   D   X

35 Once she was accepted by the youth orcestra her playing improved dramatically.
    A   B   C   D   X

36 He was constantly disappointed by the negitive attitude of the team
    A   B   C
captain, who should have known better.
    D   X

37 The friends are looking forward to their new secondary school, even though they have
    A   B   C
thorugly enjoyed their present school.
    D   X

38 They were amazed and disappointed to hear the announcement that
    A   B
their favorite player had been suspended for three matches.
    C   D   X

Please turn over

In this extract, mistakes have been made in the use of punctuation and capital letters. In your answer booklet, mark the letter where the mistake is underlined. If there isn't a mistake, mark the letter X.

The girl actually followed me up the path and stood behind me while I rang the bell.

39 She annoyed me I needed to be on my own for this. "D'you want
    A   B   C   D   X

40 something" I asked her. "My tea," she said. "And it's no good ringing the bell.
    A   B   C   D   X

41 One's out and the others in bed." "Oh." I felt completely deflated. She unlocked the door and
    A   B   C   D   X

42 I turned away. "You can come in and wait, if you want," she said.
    A   B   C
    So that was how I got into horsenose Cottage.
    D   X

43 I gazed round it, wondering which room Id been born in. It smelt of polish and flowers, and
    A   B   C   D   X

44 it was old and dark with beams across the ceiling. The walls were
    A   B
    covered with paintings of lakes and hills I wondered whether my mother had painted them.
    C   D   X

From *The Snake-Stone* by Bertie Doherty

In this extract, choose the letter below the word or words that need to be chosen for the extract to make sense and use correct English.

45 Jess had ate eated eaten ated ates the whole pizza herself.
             A   B   C   D   E

46 The pupils have wrote writed wroted written wroten postcards home to their parents.
                    A   B   C   D   E

47 Finn went timidly up too two to twose tose the door, and knocked.
                         A   B   C D   E

48 'Their is There's They'res Theres Theirs no use asking for more,' said their mother.
     A   B   C   D   E

49 They're making such a noise, no one everyone someone everybody no ones
                                 A   B   C   D   E
    could possibly hear themselves speak.

50 The children received less fewer lesser least few days off this year than last.
                            A   B   C   D   E

11+ English

Multiple-choice Test Papers
Pack 1
Test 3

Read the following carefully:

- Do not begin the test or open this booklet until told to do so
- Work as quickly and as carefully as you can
- Answers should be marked in pencil in the answer booklet provided, not in this test booklet
- You may do rough working on a separate sheet of paper
- If you make a mistake rub out the mistake and write the new answer clearly
- Be careful to keep your place in the accompanying answer booklet
- You will have 50 minutes to complete the test plus 5 minutes to read the comprehension text

OXFORD
UNIVERSITY PRESS

Great Clarendon Street, Oxford, OX2 6DP, United Kingdom

Oxford University Press is a department of the University of Oxford. It furthers the University's objective of excellence in research, scholarship, and education by publishing worldwide. Oxford is a registered trade mark of Oxford University Press in the UK and in certain other countries

Text © Sarah Lindsay 2015
Illustrations © Oxford University Press 2015

The moral rights of the author have been asserted

First published in 2015

All rights reserved. No part of this publication may be reproduced, stored in a retrieval system, or transmitted, in any form or by any means, without the prior permission in writing of Oxford University Press, or as expressly permitted by law, by licence or under terms agreed with the appropriate reprographics rights organization. Enquiries concerning reproduction outside the scope of the above should be sent to the Rights Department, Oxford University Press, at the address above.

You must not circulate this work in any other form and you must impose this same condition on any acquirer

British Library Cataloguing in Publication Data
Data available

978-0-19-274083-0

Paper used in the production of this book is a natural, recyclable product made from wood grown in sustainable forests. The manufacturing process conforms to the environmental regulations of the country of origin.

Printed in China

Acknowledgements

The publishers would like to thank the following for permissions to use copyright material:

The Reluctant Python by Gerald Durrell (from *A Zoo in My Luggage*. Reproduced with permission of Curtis Brown Group Ltd, London on behalf of the Estate of Gerald Durrell. Copyright © Gerald Durrell 1960)
A Buddhist Tale retold by John Jackman

Cover illustrations: Lo Cole

Although we have made every effort to trace and contact all copyright holders before publication this has not been possible in all cases. If notified, the publisher will rectify any errors or omissions at the earliest opportunity.

Links to third party websites are provided by Oxford in good faith and for information only. Oxford disclaims any responsibility for the materials contained in any third party website referenced in this work.

Read the extract carefully, then answer the questions in the answer booklet provided.

An enormous python has been spotted and the author, Gerald Durrell, and his friend, assisted by some local hunters, have decided to see if they can capture it ...

The path lay at first through some old native farmland, where the giant trees had been felled and now lay rotting across the ground. Between these trunks a crop of cassava had been grown and harvested, and the ground allowed to lie fallow, so that the low growth of the forest – thorn bushes, convolvulus and other tangles – had swept into the clearing and covered everything with a cloak. There was always plenty of life to be seen in these abandoned farms, and as we pushed through the intricate web of undergrowth there were birds all around us. Beautiful little fly-catchers hovered in the air, showing up powder-blue against the greenery; in the dim recesses of convolvulus-covered tree stumps robin-chats hopped perkily in search of grasshoppers, and looked startlingly like English robins; a pied crow flew from the ground ahead and flapped heavily away, crying a harsh warning; in a thicket of thorn bushes, covered with pink flowers among which zoomed big blue bees, a kurrichane treated us to a waterfall of sweet song. The path wound its way through this moist, hot, waist-high undergrowth for some time, and then quite abruptly the undergrowth ended and the path led us out onto a golden grassfield, rippling with the heat haze. We plodded across this sun-drenched expanse, the sweat pouring off us.

"I hope this damned reptile's had the sense to go to ground where there's some shade," I said to Bob. "You could fry an egg on these rocks."

Agustine, who had been padding eagerly ahead, his sarong turning from scarlet to wine-red as it absorbed the sweat from his body, turned and grinned at me, his face freckled with a mass of sweat-drops.

I followed his pointing finger and in the distance I could see an area where the rocks had been pushed up and rumpled, like bedclothes, by some ancient volcanic upheaval, so that they formed a miniature cliff running diagonally across the grassfield. On top of this I could see the figures of two more hunters, squatting patiently in the sun. When they saw us they rose to their feet and waved ferocious-looking spears in greeting.

When we reached the base of the small cliff I could see why the python had chosen this spot to stand at bay. The rock face had been split into a series of shallow caves, worn smooth by wind and water, each communicating with the other, and the whole series sloping slightly upwards into the cliff so that anything that lived in them would be in no danger of getting drowned in the rainy season. The mouth of each cave was about eight feet across, and three feet high, which gave a snake, but not much else, room for manoeuvring. The hunters had very thoughtfully set fire to all the grass in the vicinity, in an effort to smoke the reptile out. The snake had been unaffected by this, but now we had to work in a thick layer of charcoal and feathery ash up to our ankles.

Bob and I got down on our stomachs and, shoulder to shoulder, wormed our way into the mouth of the cave to try and spot the python and map out a plan of campaign. We soon found that the cave narrowed within three or four feet of the entrance so that there was only room for one person, lying as flat as he could. After the glare of the sunshine outside, the cave seemed twice as dark as it was, and we could not see a thing. The only indication that a snake was there at all was a loud peevish hissing every time we moved. We called loudly for a torch, and when this had been unpacked and handed to us we directed its beam up the narrow passage.

Eight feet ahead of us the passage ended in a circular depression in the rock, and in this the python lay coiled, shining in the torchlight as if freshly polished. It was about fifteen feet long as far as we could judge, and fat. It was also in an extremely bad temper. The longer the torch beam played on it the more prolonged and shrill did its hisses become, until they rose to an eerie shriek. We crawled out into the sunlight again and sat up.

"The thing is to get a noose round its neck, and then we can pull like hell and drag it out," said Bob.

"Yes, but the job's going to be to *get* the noose round its neck. I don't fancy being wedged in that passage if it decided to come down after me. There's no room to manoeuvre, and there's no room for anyone to help if you get entangled with it... there's only one thing to do. Agustine, go quick... quick and cut one fork-stick for me... a big one."

Presently, Agustine returned, carrying a long, straight sapling with a fork at one end. On to this fork end I fastened a slip knot with some fine cord which, the manufacturers had assured me, would stand the strain of three hundredweight. Then I unravelled fifty feet or so of the cord, and handed the rest of the coil to Agustine.

I wriggled slowly up the cave, carrying the sapling and cord with me, the torch in my mouth. The python hissed with undiminished ferocity. Then came the delicate job of trying to push the sapling ahead of me so that I could get the dangling noose over the snake's head. I found this impossible with the torch in my mouth, for at the slightest movement the beam swept everywhere but on to the point required. I put the torch on the ground, propped it up on some rocks with the beam playing on the snake and then, with infinite care, I edged the sapling up the cave towards the reptile. The python had, of course, coiled itself into a tight knot, with the head lying in the centre of the coils, so when I had got the sapling into position I had to force the snake to show its head. The only way to do this was to prod the creature vigorously with the end of the sapling.

After the first prod the shining coils seemed to swell with rage, and there came echoing down the cave a hiss so shrill and so charged with malignancy that I almost dropped the sapling. Five times I prodded before my efforts were rewarded. The python's head appeared suddenly over the top of the coils, and swept towards the end of the sapling, the mouth wide open and gleaming pinkly in the torchlight. But the movement was so sudden that I had no chance to get the noose over its head. At last, dripping with sweat, my arms aching, I crawled out into the sunlight.

"It's no good," I said to Bob. "It keeps its head buried in its coils and only pops out to strike…"

"Let me have a go," he said eagerly. "If you crawl in with me and shine the torch over my shoulder, it would help…"

The results were immediate and confusing. To our surprise the entire bulk of the snake – after a momentary resistance – slid down the cave towards us. Exhilarated, Bob shuffled backwards (thus wedging us both more tightly in the tunnel) and hauled again. The snake slid nearer and then started to unravel. Bob hauled again, and the snake uncoiled still further; its head and neck appeared out of the tangle and struck at us. Wedged like a couple of outsize sardines in an undersized can we had no room to move except backwards, and so we slid backwards on our stomachs as rapidly as we could. At last, to our relief, we reached a slight widening in the passage. Bob laid hold of the sapling and pulled at it grimly. He reminded me of a lanky and earnest blackbird tugging an outsize worm from its hole. The snake slid into view, hissing madly, its coils shuddering with muscular contraction as it tried to free itself. I crawled out rapidly.

Bob appeared at the cave mouth, scrambled to his feet and stepped back for the final jerk that would drag the snake out into the open where we could fall on it. But, as he stepped back, he put his foot on a loose rock which twisted under him, and he fell flat on his back. The sapling was jerked from his hands, the snake gave a mighty heave that freed its body and, with the smooth fluidity of water soaking into blotting paper, it slid into a crick in the cave wall that did not look as though it would accommodate a mouse. As the last four feet of its length were disappearing into the bowels of the earth, Bob and I fell on it and hung on like grim death. We could feel the rippling of the powerful muscles as the snake, buried deep in the rocky cleft, struggled to break our grip on its tail. Slowly, inch by inch, the smooth scales slipped through our sweaty hands, and then, suddenly, the snake was gone. From somewhere deep in the rocks came a triumphant hiss.

From *The Reluctant Python* by Gerald Durrell

1 How do we know the land Gerald and his friend walked across hadn't been farmed recently?

    A The land was hard and dry.
    B The weather had been too hot.
    C The native vegetation had taken hold.
    D The fences surrounding the land had been removed.
    E There were no signs of farm tools or a water supply nearby.

2 Why was the undergrowth described as being 'an intricate web'?

   A It was sticky like a spider's web.
   B It was home to many different types of animal.
   C It was dangerous and they could become trapped in it.
   D The plants in the undergrowth were the colour of a spider's web.
   E The plants wove together forming a criss-cross much like a spider's web.

3 What is convolvulus?

   A a type of bird
   B a type of tree
   C a vine-like plant
   D a farm crop
   E a type of snake

4 Which of the creatures reminded the author most of one from England?

   A a grasshopper
   B a fly-catcher
   C a pied crow
   D a robin-chat
   E a blue bee

5 Approximately how tall was the undergrowth through which the path passed?

   A about 10 cm
   B about 30 cm
   C about 1 m
   D about 5 m
   E about 10 m

6 What did Gerald Durrell mean when he said that 'you could fry an egg on these rocks' (line 16)?

   A It was very hot.
   B It would be a good location for people to camp or live.
   C The rocks were too dangerous for them to climb.
   D They had time to stop and prepare lunch.
   E The rocks were flat and smooth like a frying pan.

7–8 Which two descriptions of Agustine in the extract show that he was feeling very hot?

   A His face was red.
   B His clothes were damp.
   C He put on a hat to protect himself from the sun.
   D He was drinking water.
   E He had sweat-drops on his face.

9 Why were there two men on the ridge (lines 22–24)?

   A They were protecting their land.
   B They were there to help track the python.
   C They were looking for water.
   D They were burning scrubland to make it suitable for planting crops.
   E They were interested to see what Gerald Durrell and his friend were doing.

10–11 According to Gerald Durrell, what were two reasons the caves were a good shelter for snakes?

   A They would stay dry during the wet weather.
   B They were close to a stream.
   C The entrance was quite narrow, which would make it difficult for a predator to enter the cave.
   D They would allow the snake to see a potential enemy approaching from a long way off.
   E They stayed warm at night.

Continue to the next page

12 What is meant by the phrase 'wormed our way into the mouth of the cave…' (lines 33–34)?
  A ran
  B dug
  C crept
  D walked
  E squirmed

13 Why did it seem so dark in the cave?
  A The candles they had taken in had gone out.
  B The grey, charcoal walls of the cave made everything look black.
  C They couldn't open their eyes properly because of the dust.
  D People were standing by the entrance and blocking the light.
  E Their eyes were accustomed to the bright sunshine.

14 Which phrase most accurately describes the python?
  A small and frightened
  B sleek, shiny and gentle
  C thin and angry
  D large, angry, shiny
  E fat, good-natured, glossy

15 What made the snake let out an eerie shriek?
  A being prodded with the stick
  B seeing the men try to enter the cave
  C being blinded with the torchlight
  D fear that it was being trapped
  E being hit by a falling boulder

16 What is the most likely reason Gerald asked Agustine particularly to select a *big* sapling?
  A because he was concerned that a small one might break
  B because he didn't want to get too close to the python
  C because it needed to extend to the entrance of the cave
  D because the two friends were using it together
  E because he wanted to lean on it as he moved deeper into the cave

17 What is the python's first response to Gerald entering the cave with the sapling?
  A to raise its head
  B to strike and try to bite him
  C to hide in a crack in the cave wall
  D to try to go past him and leave the cave
  E to go into a position to protect itself

18 Why are the friends likened to sardines?
  A because they are hot and smelly
  B because they are sweating and slippery to the touch
  C because they look a greyish colour
  D because they are tightly jammed together in a small space
  E because they are lying on their stomachs

19 What is meant by the description of the python looking as if it had been 'freshly polished' (line 41)?
  A wet
  B patterned
  C light in colour
  D shiny and smooth
  E dull and dark

Please turn over

20 Which action by Bob reminded Gerald of a blackbird?
  A becoming stuck in the cave
  B sliding on his stomach
  C trying to pull the snake from the cave
  D falling to the rocks
  E crawling backwards down the cave

21 What caused Bob to fall over?
  A He fainted with the heat.
  B He sprained his knee.
  C He stood on a loose rock.
  D He stumbled over the sapling.
  E He slipped as he tried to run away.

22–23 Which two reasons explain why the two friends couldn't prevent the python escaping?
  A It was too powerful to hold.
  B It threatened to bite them.
  C It was too quick for them to grab.
  D They could not get a good grip on it.
  E The hunters told them to leave it alone.

24 The area described in the extract is most like:
  A a desert
  B a village
  C a jungle
  D a city
  E a swamp

25 What is suggested by the last line in the extract?
  A The python had defeated the men.
  B The men were close to capturing the python.
  C The python was trapped and had nowhere to hide.
  D The men had successfully moved the python to where they wanted it to go.
  E The python was trying to slide past the men and escape from the cave.

Answer these questions about the meanings of words or phrases as they are used in the extract.

26 The ground was allowed to 'lie fallow'. What does 'fallow' mean (line 3)?
  A stony
  B planted with crops
  C left without having crop seeds planted
  D planted with shrubs and trees
  E set aside for farm animals to graze

27 What is the closest meaning to 'undiminished' (line 55)?
  A not very bright
  B no less
  C nearly complete
  D greater
  E determined

28 Look at lines 72–73. What does 'momentary' mean?
  A stubborn
  B stiff
  C strong
  D determined
  E temporary

Continue to the next page

29 Which of the options below is not a possible definition for 'exhilarated' (line 73)?

    A made lively
    B being cheerful
    C showing considerable excitement
    D concerned and anxious
    E being elated

30 The words below are found in the extract. Which is the pronoun?

    A but
    B as
    C he
    D stepped
    E back

31 Which of these lines from the extract includes a metaphor?

    A through this hot, moist, waist-high undergrowth
    B where the rocks had been pushed up and rumpled, like bedclothes
    C It was about fifteen feet long
    D and other tangles had swept into the clearing and covered everything with a cloak
    E a long, straight sapling with a fork at one end

32 Which of these words from the extract is a proper noun?

Presently, Agustine returned, carrying a long, straight sapling with a fork at one end.
  A   B   C   D   E

In these sentences there are a number of spelling mistakes. Choose the letter where the spelling mistake is underlined or, if there isn't a spelling mistake, choose the letter X.

33 Most of the farmers were unable to afford the basic machinary that
    A   B   C
would have improved their productivity.
    D   X

34 The young ranger protested his inocence when accused of poaching.
    A   B   C   D   X

35 The tourists were impatent to get started on their safari trip to a famous waterhole.
    A   B   C   D   X

36 A rather unpleasant government offical was insisting that
    A   B
he checked everyone's passport and documentation.
    C   D   X

37 They finally left their accomodation just before nine o'clock,
    A   B   C
considerably later than originally intended.
    D   X

38 When eventually they reached the waterhole the ranger was delighted
    A   B
to anounce the rare deer he had refered to earlier were thought to be coming in our direction.
    C   D   X

Please turn over

In this extract mistakes have been made in the use of punctuation and capital letters. In your answer booklet, mark the letter where the mistake is underlined. If there isn't a mistake, mark the letter X.

This story from the Buddhist faith is about a King teaching his wise men a lesson...

39 The fourth blind man felt the elephant's leg. "It is obvious that this elephant is like a tree."
    A   B   C
when the fifth blind man caught hold
D   X

40 of the elephant's tail he was absolutely convinced that the elephant was like a rope.
    A   B
Many other blind men felt the elephant and each had his own idea as to what it was like.
C   D   X

41 Soon, quarrels broke out. Angry words were shouted One man pushed another.
    A   B   C   D   X

42 The quarrels turned into fights as each blind man was sure he was right.
    A   B
The wise men looked on in amazement at the way the blind men were behaving.
C
some of them even began to laugh.
D   X

43 "Why are you laughing? enquired the King. "The way
    A   B
these blind men are behaving is no different to how you behave!"
C   D   X

44 "You are always quarrelling because you cannot see anyone elses point of view."
    A   B   C   D   X

From *A Buddhist Tale* retold by John Jackman

In this extract, choose the letter below the word or words that need to be chosen for the extract to make sense and use correct English.

45 How sure are you that their there they're there's they's coming today?
                                        A B   C   D   E

46 "It would be cool if you and I me us we all could meet later," she said.
                                                 AB C D E

47 Their was There's Their were There was There were tall, beautiful hardwood trees
    A   B   C   D   E
which grew there before being illegally felled.

48 "This is the baddest worst worstest worse worsest example of behaviour I've seen
                  A   B   C   D   E
for many years," shouted the teacher.

49 The lads were disappointed they'd lost the game, for every one of them
done had done had did has did done did his best.
A   B   C   D   E

50 The survivors in the lifeboat had not had no none any nothing not water for days.
                                                     A B C   D   E

11+ English

Multiple-choice Test Papers
Pack 1
Test 4

Read the following carefully:

- Do not begin the test or open this booklet until told to do so
- Work as quickly and as carefully as you can
- Answers should be marked in pencil in the answer booklet provided, not in this test booklet
- You may do rough working on a separate sheet of paper
- If you make a mistake rub out the mistake and write the new answer clearly
- Be careful to keep your place in the accompanying answer booklet
- You will have 50 minutes to complete the test plus 5 minutes to read the comprehension text

OXFORD
UNIVERSITY PRESS

Great Clarendon Street, Oxford, OX2 6DP, United Kingdom

Oxford University Press is a department of the University of Oxford. It furthers the University's objective of excellence in research, scholarship, and education by publishing worldwide. Oxford is a registered trade mark of Oxford University Press in the UK and in certain other countries

Text © Sarah Lindsay 2015
Illustrations © Oxford University Press 2015

The moral rights of the author have been asserted

First published in 2015

All rights reserved. No part of this publication may be reproduced, stored in a retrieval system, or transmitted, in any form or by any means, without the prior permission in writing of Oxford University Press, or as expressly permitted by law, by licence or under terms agreed with the appropriate reprographics rights organization. Enquiries concerning reproduction outside the scope of the above should be sent to the Rights Department, Oxford University Press, at the address above.

You must not circulate this work in any other form and you must impose this same condition on any acquirer

British Library Cataloguing in Publication Data
Data available

978-0-19-274083-0

Paper used in the production of this book is a natural, recyclable product made from wood grown in sustainable forests. The manufacturing process conforms to the environmental regulations of the country of origin.

Printed in China

Acknowledgements

The publishers would like to thank the following for permissions to use copyright material:

The National Archives Learning Curve, www.learningcurve.gov.uk
The Adventures of Tom Sawyer, by Mark Twain

Cover illustrations: Lo Cole

Although we have made every effort to trace and contact all copyright holders before publication this has not been possible in all cases. If notified, the publisher will rectify any errors or omissions at the earliest opportunity.

Links to third party websites are provided by Oxford in good faith and for information only. Oxford disclaims any responsibility for the materials contained in any third party website referenced in this work.

Read the extract carefully, then answer the questions in the answer booklet provided.

Martin Luther King Jr. was born in Atlanta, Georgia on 15th January, 1929. Both his father and grandfather were Baptist preachers who had been actively involved in the civil rights movement. King graduated from Morehouse College in 1948. After considering careers in medicine and law, he entered the ministry.

While studying at Crozer Theological Seminary in Pennsylvania, King heard a lecture on Mahatma 5
Gandhi and the non-violent civil disobedience campaign that he used successfully against British rule in India. King read several books on the ideas of Gandhi, and eventually became convinced that the same methods could be employed by blacks to obtain civil rights in America. He was particularly struck by Gandhi's words: "Through our pain we will make them see their injustice." King was also influenced by Henry David Thoreau and his theories on how to use non-violent resistance to achieve 10
social change.

After his marriage to Coretta Scott, King became pastor of the Dexter Avenue Baptist Church in Montgomery, Alabama. In Montgomery, like most towns in the Deep South, buses were segregated. On 1st December, 1955, Rosa Parks, a middle-aged tailor's assistant, who was tired after a hard day's work, refused to give up her seat to a white man. 15

After the arrest of Rosa Parks, King and his friends, Ralph David Abernathy, Edgar Nixon, and Bayard Rustin helped organise protests against bus segregation. It was decided that black people in Montgomery would refuse to use the buses until passengers were completely integrated. King was arrested and his house was fire-bombed. Others involved in the Montgomery Bus Boycott also suffered from harassment and intimidation, but the protest continued. 20

For thirteen months the 17,000 black people in Montgomery walked to work or obtained lifts from the small car-owning black population of the city. Eventually, the loss of revenue and a decision by the Supreme Court forced the Montgomery Bus Company to accept integration, and the boycott came to an end on 20th December, 1956.

In 1957 King joined with the Reverend Ralph David Abernathy and Bayard Rustin to form the 25
Southern Christian Leadership Conference (SCLC). The new organisation was committed to using non-violence in the struggle for civil rights, and SCLC adopted the motto: "Not one hair of one head of one person should be harmed."

After the successful outcome of the Montgomery Bus Boycott, King wrote *Stride Toward Freedom* (1958). The book described what happened at Montgomery and explained King's views on non- 30
violence and direct action. *Stride Toward Freedom* was to have a considerable influence on the civil rights movement.

In Greensboro, North Carolina, a small group of black students read the book and decided to take action themselves. They started a student sit-in at the restaurant of their local Woolworth's store which had a policy of not serving black people. In the days that followed they were joined by other 35
black students until they occupied all the seats in the restaurant. The students were often physically assaulted, but following the teachings of King they did not hit back.

King's non-violent strategy was adopted by black students all over the Deep South. This included the activities of the Freedom Riders in their campaign against segregated transport. Within six months these sit-ins had ended restaurant and lunch-counter segregation in twenty-six southern 40
cities. Student sit-ins were also successful against segregation in public parks, swimming pools, theatres, churches, libraries, museums and beaches.

King travelled the country making speeches and inspiring people to become involved in the civil rights movement. As well as advocating non-violent student sit-ins, King also urged economic boycotts similar to the one that took place at Montgomery. He argued that as African Americans 45
made up 10% of the population they had considerable economic power. By selective buying, they could reward companies that were sympathetic to the civil rights movement while punishing those who still segregated their workforce.

The campaign to end segregation at lunch counters in Birmingham, Alabama, was less successful. In the spring of 1963 police turned dogs and fire hoses on the demonstrators. King and 50
a large number of his supporters, including schoolchildren, were arrested and jailed.

King always stressed the importance of the ballot. He argued that once all African Americans had the vote they would become an important political force. Although they were a minority, once the vote was organised, they could determine the result of presidential and state elections. This was illustrated by the African American support for John F. Kennedy that helped give him a narrow victory in the 1960 election.

During the 1960 presidential election campaign John F. Kennedy argued for a new Civil Rights Act. After the election it was discovered that over 70 per cent of the African American vote went to Kennedy. However, during the first two years of his presidency, Kennedy failed to put forward his promised legislation.

The Civil Rights bill was brought before Congress in 1963 and in a speech on television on 11th June, Kennedy pointed out that: "The Negro baby born in America today, regardless of the section of the nation in which he is born, has about one-half as much chance of completing high school as a white baby born in the same place on the same day; one-third as much chance of completing college; one-third as much chance of becoming a professional man; twice as much chance of becoming unemployed; about one-seventh as much chance of earning $10,000 a year; a life expectancy which is seven years shorter; and the prospects of earning only half as much."

In an attempt to persuade Congress to pass Kennedy's proposed legislation, King and other civil rights leaders organised the famous March on Washington for Jobs and Freedom. Bayard Rustin was given overall control of the march and he managed to persuade the leaders of all the various civil rights groups to participate in the planned protest meeting at the Lincoln Memorial.

On 28th August, 1963 King delivered his famous *I have a dream…* speech.

I say to you today, my friends, so even though we face the difficulties of today and tomorrow, I still have a dream. It is a dream deeply rooted in the American dream.

I have a dream that one day this nation will rise up and live out the true meaning of its creed: "We hold these truths to be self-evident, that all men are created equal."

I have a dream that one day on the red hills of Georgia, the sons of former slaves and the sons of former slave owners will be able to sit down together at the table of brotherhood.

I have a dream that one day even the state of Mississippi, a state sweltering with the heat of injustice, sweltering with the heat of oppression, will be transformed into an oasis of freedom and justice.

I have a dream that my four little children will one day live in a nation where they will not be judged by the colour of their skin but by the content of their character. I have a dream today.

I have a dream that one day down in Alabama, with its vicious racists, with its governor having his lips dripping with the words of "interposition" and "nullification", one day right there in Alabama little black boys and black girls will be able to join hands with little white boys and white girls as sisters and brothers. I have a dream today.

I have a dream that one day every valley shall be exalted, every hill and mountain shall be made low, the rough places will be made plain, and the crooked places will be made straight, and the glory of the Lord shall be revealed, and all flesh shall see it together.

This is our hope. This is the faith that I go back to the South with. With this faith we will be able to hew out of the mountain of despair a stone of hope. With this faith we will be able to transform the jangling discords of our nation into a beautiful symphony of brotherhood. With this faith we will be able to work together, to pray together, to struggle together, to go to jail together, to stand up for freedom together, knowing that we will be free one day.

And when this happens, when we allow freedom to ring, when we let it ring from every village and every hamlet, from every state and every city, we will be able to speed up that day when all of God's children, black men and white men, Jews and Gentiles, Protestants and Catholics, will be able to join hands and sing in the words of the old Negro spiritual: Free at last! Free at last! Thank God Almighty, we are free at last!

He continued to work tirelessly for the equality of all races. In December 1964 Martin Luther King Jr. received the Nobel Peace Prize.

On 3rd April 1968 he made his last speech, *I've been to the mountain top…*; the following day he was assassinated by a gunman on the balcony of the Lorraine Motel in Memphis, Tennessee.

Source: The National Archives Learning Curve; *www.learningcurve.gov.uk*

1 In which decade was Martin Luther King Jr. born?
  A 1900s
  B 1910s
  C 1920s
  D 1930s
  E 1940s

2 Which of the people listed below probably influenced Martin Luther King Jr. to study religion rather than medicine or law?
  A Mahatma Gandhi
  B Henry David Thoreau
  C Coretta Scott, his wife
  D Ralph David Abernathy
  E his father and grandfather

3 Based on the information in the extract, whose ideas *most* influenced the way Martin Luther King Jr. would seek to achieve justice?
  A his teachers
  B Rosa Parks
  C Mahatma Gandhi
  D Henry David Thoreau
  E Ralph David Abernathy

4 What was the main way Martin Luther King Jr. planned to get equal rights for black people in the United States?
  A by asking for help from international organisations
  B by running for government office himself
  C by organising peaceful protests
  D by going on a hunger strike
  E by writing new laws

5 Why did Rosa Parks have such an important role in the equal rights protests?
  A She was good at organising demonstrations.
  B She took a stand against discrimination that encouraged other people to do the same.
  C She was a friend of Martin Luther King Jr. and helped him in many ways.
  D She knew people working in the government and was able to go to them for assistance.
  E She was good at writing and making speeches.

6 In the first protest organised by King and his friends in Montgomery, what did they ask black people to do?
  A go into shops that only served white people
  B refuse to go to work
  C refuse to travel by bus
  D block roads so people couldn't travel
  E take seats in restaurants that only served white people

7 How long did the bus boycott last?
  A about a week
  B about a month
  C a little less than a year
  D a little more than a year
  E about two years

8–9 Which <u>two</u> factors were most significant in leading to the end of the bus boycott?
  A The bus company lowered its prices.
  B The police insisted people use the buses.
  C The bus company was losing money.
  D Black people became tired of walking to work and began to take the buses again.
  E The government made it illegal for the bus company to continue segregation.

Continue to the next page

10 What was an immediate effect of King's book *Stride Towards Freedom*?
  A Other people were influenced to take action.
  B He was arrested and forced to go to trial.
  C He won an award and became well known.
  D He started the Southern Christian Leadership Conference.
  E He was asked by the government to help them improve the rights of black Americans.

11 In the context of this extract, what is meant by 'economic boycotts' (lines 44–45)?
  A only buying goods made in other countries
  B refusing to sell to certain companies
  C demanding higher pay
  D refusing to buy or use goods or services from certain companies
  E refusing to work

12 Which of these was the most important way by which King thought he could encourage the government to support civil rights?
  A by talking to politicians
  B by encouraging politicians to read his book
  C by persuading black people to vote for politicians who promised to support civil rights
  D by telling black people not to pay their taxes
  E by encouraging people to vote only for black politicians

13 Why might some black people who had voted for President Kennedy have been disappointed by him?
  A He decided not to support civil rights.
  B He was very slow introducing laws against segregation.
  C He didn't appoint any black politicians.
  D He refused to meet with Martin Luther King Jr.
  E He stated that enough was already being done to further civil rights.

14–15 What are the two main reasons few young black people were getting good, well-paid jobs when they left school?
  A They were often less well educated.
  B The higher paying jobs were in parts of the country in which few black Americans lived.
  C Some white employers gave preference to white applicants for jobs.
  D Many young black Americans were interested in professions that did not pay well.
  E Many black Americans went on after school to work in a family business.

16 How did King help President Kennedy persuade Congress to pass the Civil Rights Bill?
  A He gave a speech to Congress.
  B He encouraged people to write to their government leaders.
  C He organised bus boycotts across the country.
  D He arranged a mass meeting of people in Washington, D.C.
  E He urged all black workers to go on strike.

17 At what time of year did Martin Luther King Jr. deliver his famous *I have a dream…* speech?
  A spring
  B summer
  C autumn
  D winter
  E new year

18 What was King's central belief that governed all he did to promote civil rights?
  A All people are created equal and should be treated as such.
  B All parts of life in the United States needed to change.
  C Poor people should pay less tax.
  D Most people were not doing enough to help others.
  E White and black people should live separate lives.

19 Using clues in the extract, from which country did the ancestors of most of the black Americans at this time come from?
  A Asia
  B Europe
  C South America
  D Africa
  E Australia

20 How did King want all people to be judged?
  A by the type of job they held
  B by where they lived
  C by the amount of education they have received
  D by whether they are a good person
  E by the amount of money they earned

21 In what year was King assassinated?
  A 1958
  B 1960
  C 1963
  D 1964
  E 1968

22 Which of these lines from the extract best show the difficulties King and his followers were up against in their fight for equal rights?
  A Lines 7–9
  B Lines 21–22
  C Lines 35–36
  D Lines 41–42
  E Lines 50–51

23 Why did King repeat the phrase 'I have a dream' in his speech?
  A He wanted the lines in his speech to rhyme.
  B He felt that people would not understand what he meant the first time he said it.
  C He was addressing a large audience and wanted to make sure that if people missed the phrase the first time they would have other chances to hear it.
  D He believed that a repetition of the phrase would have a great impact on the people listening and would make the speech memorable.
  E He repeated many phrases in the speech.

24 How was Martin Luther King Jr. honoured for his work?
  A He was knighted.
  B He became a lord.
  C He was chosen to work with the president.
  D He was given the Nobel Peace Prize.
  E He was made mayor of Washington, D.C.

25 What type of writing is this extract?
  A a tale
  B a myth
  C a biography
  D a piece of fiction
  E an autobiography

Answer these questions about the meanings of words or phrases as they are used in the extract.

26 'Through our pain we will make them see their injustice.' What does 'injustice' mean (line 9)?
  A unfairness
  B illegality
  C irresponsibility
  D unkindness
  E truthfulness

27 What is the closest meaning to 'segregated' (line 13)?
- A put together
- B merged
- C set apart
- D crowded
- E out-of-bounds

28 'King's non-violent strategy was adopted…' (line 38). What does 'strategy' mean?
- A idea
- B thought
- C attitude
- D feeling
- E plan

29 Which of the options below is not a possible definition for 'participate' (line 71)?
- A take part
- B stand back from
- C be involved
- D share in
- E attend

Answer the following questions about these words and phrases.

30 Which word in this phrase is an adjective?

'the red hills of Georgia…'
- A the
- B red
- C hills
- D of
- E Georgia

31 Which of these lines from the extract includes a metaphor?
- A who was tired after a hard day's work
- B the small car-owning black population
- C will be transformed into an oasis of freedom and justice
- D King travelled the country making speeches
- E the prospects of earning only half as much

32 Which of these words from the extract is a connective?

<u>The</u> <u>students</u> <u>were</u> often physically assaulted, <u>but</u> <u>following</u> the teachings
A   B   C   D   E

In these sentences there are a number of spelling mistakes. Choose the letter where the spelling mistake is underlined or, if there isn't a spelling mistake, choose the letter X.

33 <u>King heard</u> <u>a lecture on</u> <u>Mahatma Gandhi and</u> <u>the non-violent civil disobedience campain.</u>
     A   **B**   **C**   **D**   **X**

34 <u>King read several books</u> <u>on the ideas of Gandhi,</u> <u>and eventually became convinced that</u>
     A   **B**   **C**

<u>the same methods could be employed.</u>
D   **X**

35 <u>He was particully struck</u> <u>by Gandhi's words,</u> <u>'Through our pain we will make them</u>
     A   **B**   **C**

<u>see their injustice.'</u>
D   **X**

Please turn over

36	King was also influenced by Henry David Thoreau and his theories
	A B
	on how to use non-violent resistance to acheive social change.
	C D X

37	After his marrage to Coretta Scott, King became pastor of the
	A B C
	Dexter Avenue Baptist Church.
	D X

38	Rosa Parks, a middle-aged tailor's assistent, who was tired after a hard day's work,
	A B
	refused to give up her seat to a white man.
	C D X

In this extract mistakes have been made in the use of punctuation and capital letters. Choose the letter where the mistake is or, if there isn't a mistake, choose the letter X.

39	Sid flew downstairs, and said, Oh, Aunt Polly, come! Tom's dying."
	A B C D X

40	"Dying?" "Yes'm. Don't wait – come quick!" "Rubbish! I don't believe it"
	A B C D X

41	But she fled upstairs nevertheless with Sid and Mary at her heels. And her face grew white, too.
	A B C D X

42	her lip trembled. When she reached the bedside she gasped out, "You Tom!
	A B C
	Tom, what's the matter with you?"
	D X

43	"Oh, Auntie, I'm –" "What's the matter with you, child" "Oh, Auntie, my sore toe's mortified!"
	A B C D X

44	The old lady sank in her chair and laughed a little, then cried a little, then did both together.
	A B C D X

From *The Adventures of Tom Sawyer* by Mark Twain

In these sentences, choose the letter below the word or words that need to be chosen for the extract to make sense and use correct English.

45	The manager said they did well done well done good did good did we'll in the last match.
	A B C D E

46	"Ask your mum if we us two you and me us we's can go to the cinema," she said.
	A B C D E

47	They weren't sure wether whether weather wheather wetter the rain would stop.
	A B C D E

48	"This is the beautifullest more beautiful most beautiful most beautifullest beautiful
	A B C D E
	of the two dolls.

49	The rider slipped and lost the rein rain reign rhein raine.
	A B C D E

50	"That is none appropriate inappropriate unappropriate nonappropriate misappropriate
	A B C D E
	so far as I'm concerned," he stressed.

11+
English

Writing Tasks – Multiple-choice Test Papers
Pack 1

Read the following carefully:

- You may write your answers in pencil or pen
- You may do rough planning on a separate piece of paper
- Keep the word limit in mind as you are completing a task
- If you make a mistake, cross or rub it out and then continue writing
- Read the relevant comprehension text in the test papers before starting a task
- You will have up to 10 minutes reading time and then a further 30 minutes to complete a task

OXFORD
UNIVERSITY PRESS

Great Clarendon Street, Oxford, OX2 6DP, United Kingdom

Oxford University Press is a department of the University of Oxford. It furthers the University's objective of excellence in research, scholarship, and education by publishing worldwide. Oxford is a registered trade mark of Oxford University Press in the UK and in certain other countries

Text © Sarah Lindsay 2015
Illustrations © Oxford University Press 2015

The moral rights of the author have been asserted

First published in 2015

All rights reserved. No part of this publication may be reproduced, stored in a retrieval system, or transmitted, in any form or by any means, without the prior permission in writing of Oxford University Press, or as expressly permitted by law, by licence or under terms agreed with the appropriate reprographics rights organization. Enquiries concerning reproduction outside the scope of the above should be sent to the Rights Department, Oxford University Press, at the address above.

You must not circulate this work in any other form and you must impose this same condition on any acquirer

British Library Cataloguing in Publication Data
Data available

978-0-19-274083-0

Paper used in the production of this book is a natural, recyclable product made from wood grown in sustainable forests. The manufacturing process conforms to the environmental regulations of the country of origin.

Printed in China

Acknowledgements

The publishers would like to thank the following for permissions to use copyright material:

Cover illustrations: Lo Cole

Although we have made every effort to trace and contact all copyright holders before publication this has not been possible in all cases. If notified, the publisher will rectify any errors or omissions at the earliest opportunity.

Links to third party websites are provided by Oxford in good faith and for information only. Oxford disclaims any responsibility for the materials contained in any third party website referenced in this work.

Writing Task A

Read the extract from The Silver Sword *in Test 1 before completing this task.*

Statement A: Ruth and Bronia should continue living in the forest as they had done before Edek was captured.

Statement B: Ruth and Bronia should try to find their mother.

The statements above represent two sides of a debate about what Ruth and Bronia should do now that Edek has been captured. Which statement do you think is right? Explain your answer. Write no more than 250 words.

Writing Task B

Read the extract from Around the World in 80 Days *in Test 2 before completing this task.*

Imagine that you are Michael Palin on your journey around the world. Write a letter to the leader of a government asking permission to visit his or her country. (The country can be fictional.)

You should:

- explain who you are
- describe the journey you are undertaking
- give the reasons why you wish to visit this particular country
- use a standard letter format

Write no more than 250 words.

Writing Task C

Read the extract from The Reluctant Python *in Test 3 before completing this task.*

Gerald Durrell tells his story using evocative, descriptive language. Continue the text, writing no more than 250 words. Be creative, but follow the author's writing style.

Writing Task D

Read the extract about Martin Luther King Jr. in Test 4 before completing this task.

Write an account of an occasion when you stood up in front of a crowd. An example might be when you had to give a speech or presentation, or participated in a school assembly or performance.

Include details of:

- where and when the event took place
- the audience
- the aim or purpose of the event
- how you felt during the experience

Write no more than 250 words.

11+ English

Multiple-choice Test Papers
Pack 1
Answer sheets

The answer sheets for Bond 11+ Test papers English: Pack 1 Multiple-choice version are in this booklet. Please ensure you are using the correct answer sheet for the test you are taking.

OXFORD
UNIVERSITY PRESS

Great Clarendon Street, Oxford, OX2 6DP, United Kingdom

Oxford University Press is a department of the University of Oxford. It furthers the University's objective of excellence in research, scholarship, and education by publishing worldwide. Oxford is a registered trade mark of Oxford University Press in the UK and in certain other countries

© Sarah Lindsay 2015
Illustrations © Oxford University Press 2015

The moral rights of the author have been asserted

First published in 2015

All rights reserved. No part of this publication may be reproduced, stored in a retrieval system, or transmitted, in any form or by any means, without the prior permission in writing of Oxford University Press, or as expressly permitted by law, by licence or under terms agreed with the appropriate reprographics rights organization. Enquiries concerning reproduction outside the scope of the above should be sent to the Rights Department, Oxford University Press, at the address above.

You must not circulate this work in any other form and you must impose this same condition on any acquirer

British Library Cataloguing in Publication Data
Data available

978-0-19-274083-0

Paper used in the production of this book is a natural, recyclable product made from wood grown in sustainable forests. The manufacturing process conforms to the environmental regulations of the country of origin.

Printed in China

Acknowledgements

The publishers would like to thank the following for permissions to use copyright material:

Cover illustrations: Lo Cole

Although we have made every effort to trace and contact all copyright holders before publication this has not been possible in all cases. If notified, the publisher will rectify any errors or omissions at the earliest opportunity.

Links to third party websites are provided by Oxford in good faith and for information only. Oxford disclaims any responsibility for the materials contained in any third party website referenced in this work.

Bond 11+ English Test 1

Name

Bond 11+ English Test 2

Name:

Bond 11+ English Test 3

Name

Bond 11+ English Test 4

Name:

Notes

Notes

Notes